# smallspaces

# smallspaces

### making the most of the space you have

**REBECCA TANQUERAY**

*photography by* **Chris Everard**

RYLAND
PETERS
& SMALL

LONDON  NEW YORK

First published in the United States in 2003 by
Ryland Peters & Small, Inc.
519 Broadway
5th Floor
New York NY10012
www.rylandpeters.com

10 9 8 7 6 5 4 3 2

Library of Congress Cataloging-in-Publication Data

Tanqueray, Rebecca.
 Small spaces : making the most of the space you
have / Rebecca Tanqueray with photography by
Chris Everard.
     p. cm.
Includes index.
 ISBN 1-84172-414-9
 1.  Small houses. 2.  Interior decoration.  I. Everard,
Chris. II.
Title.
 NA7115 .T26 2003
 747'.8837--dc21

                                    2002014395

Printed and bound in China

**senior editor** Clare Double
**location research** Claire Hector
**production** Patricia Harrington

**art director** Gabriella Le Grazie
**publishing director** Alison Starling

**plans by** Russell Bell

# contents

# introduction

Too many of us, these days, have too little space. With house prices in some areas escalating beyond our budgets, it's no surprise that we find ourselves squeezed into homes we've outgrown or forced to live somewhere smaller than we would like. Half the problem, of course, is that we have come to expect something more for our money. Bombarded by the media with images of loft apartments and giant open-plan living spaces, we are no longer content with our tiny homes, which—by comparison—seem cramped and claustrophobic.

Living in a small space, however, need not be a negative experience. Think of the Japanese, who have made an art out of it and who relish the positives of diminutive design. Approaching the space problem intelligently, they have come up with solutions that are compact and flexible, creating homes—or, at the extreme, capsule living spaces—that function brilliantly despite their size.

Here, too, we can do the same, and in this book I hope to encourage you to look again at your home—whether it is an urban pad or a country cottage—and to think of ways of overcoming its limitations. Of course, if you have the means, you may be able to change your space structurally by extending up or out, or by knocking down walls to open up the interior. If this is not an option, however, there are many other methods of improving the feel of your home, by rearranging its layout, perhaps; investing in a few key pieces of furniture; or even just a new coat of paint.

Browse through the case studies at the front of the book for inspiration. While at first sight some of them may seem far removed from your living quarters, all of them—from the dynamic mini skyscraper to the triangular Paris apartment— illustrate countless innovative and accessible ways in which you can make the most of your space and offer ingenious ideas that have universal relevance. I've extrapolated the best of these in the second two sections—The Zones and Solutions—to show you just how easy it is to apply space-saving principles to every bit of your own home.

Who wants a loft when you can live somewhere compact, comfortable, and cozy? Small spaces are the next big thing.

# making the most of your space

Once an open space, the studio is now a multi-functional home. A mezzanine level was erected to serve as the "bedroom" and give access to a rooftop terrace. Exploiting vertical space like this is a good way of creating more room in any small home, as long as the ceilings are high enough.

LEFT The floor has been topped with resin and marble "pebbles" throughout, giving the place the feel of an urban beach house. This not only adds a good dose of textural interest to the otherwise neutral interior, it is also highly practical, providing the perfect hard-wearing party-proof surface.

# mezzanine
## magic

Most of us, when we buy a home, know just what we are getting: three bedrooms, one bathroom, or whatever. Fashion photographer Guy Hills, however, had no such readymade interior when he bought this old mews house in north London. A small two-story building with unexpectedly high ceilings, it seemed perfect for a live-work space. The first floor (undivided but for a couple of small rooms at the back) was just the place for Hills's photographic studio; upstairs—one large, undivided room with windows at front and back—could be his home.

Building an interior from scratch can be daunting, but it offers the opportunity to create somewhere tailormade, somewhere that can accommodate just what you want, just where you want it. This is all very well and good in a large space, but in a small one it can prove more of a challenge—particularly if, like Hills, you have big plans. Hills wanted his studio home to have all the usual living areas, but he wanted something more besides. "I like a fairly minimal look," he explains, "so I needed acres of storage space. And I entertain a lot, so I needed room for lots of people."

The living "room" is defined only by its furniture: a curvy 1970s sofa, an armchair, a coffee table. Simple and masculine, this space is flexible enough to double as a meeting room when clients are visiting.

To help him turn his one room into a multi-functional living space, he called in the experts, designer Maria Speake and architect Joanna Rippon. Realizing they had no chance of squeezing everything onto one floor, their first trick was to add an extra level—a mezzanine—to accommodate a sleeping area. Suspended from the ceiling, the structure is just big enough for a bed, its metal frame cleverly doubling as the bed surround. Adding a mezzanine was an ingenious solution to the

## The giant skylight allows light to flood into the interior and also provides a gateway to Hills's tiny roof terrace beyond.

space problem, not only because it took the "bedroom" out of the main floor, freeing space for eating and entertaining, but also because it helped to define the areas beneath. Its chunky staircase splits the room in two, separating the kitchen and bathroom on one side from the living room and office on the other.

Mezzanines, of course, are only effective if you have high ceilings to play with. Even here, although there is plenty of room underneath the structure, space above is tight. Sitting up in bed is possible; standing is more difficult, unless the giant skylight, installed right above the bed, is open. Operated by remote control, this huge window allows light to flood into the interior and also provides a gateway to Hills's tiny roof terrace beyond. There's another bonus to this feature, too. By creating a see-through ceiling for the "bedroom" (with views of sky and stars, of course), the designers cleverly avoided any claustrophobia that might have come from sleeping in such a shallow space. (Blackout and heat-diffusing blinds mean Hills can control temperature and light.)

OPPOSITE **Above the mezzanine bed deck, the designers installed a giant skylight. This provides access to Hills's tiny rooftop terrace and makes the shallow sleeping space seem a lot less claustrophobic, as well as lighting the whole interior.**

THIS PAGE **Brilliantly neat and compact, the office is tucked beneath the mezzanine. It comprises, simply, a row of units topped with sleek reclaimed mahogany.**

The work station includes everything you could ask for: built-in wall lights; copious amounts of storage space; a built-in (but shut away) lightbox.

office

bedroom (mezzanine level)

kitchen

bathroom

living room

stairs to first floor

Beneath the mezzanine is the office, a neat row of "floating" white units topped with a reclaimed mahogany worktop. This continues beyond the units to form an integral desk at one end, so Hills has no need for any extraneous furniture. The work station includes everything you could ask for: built-in wall lights (again, no need for clutter-inducing freestanding lamps); copious amounts of storage space; a built-in (but shut away) lightbox. There is even space for a plasma-screen television, just in case Hills saves up enough money to buy one.

Opposite the office is the living "room"—a giant 1970s leather sofa that curves languidly around the walls, an armchair, a cowhide rug, and a smoked-glass coffee table. Defined only by the furniture, this area is flexible enough to double as a meeting room when Hills sees clients and provides plenty of seating for parties.

At the other end of the room is the kitchen and a small bathroom, which is tucked (almost invisibly) behind a white door. The kitchen, which—after all—takes up virtually half of the floor space, feels capacious with its line of white units and semi-see-through furniture. The tour de force here, however, is the amount of ingenious built-in storage, cleverly designed so you don't even realize it's there. The refrigerator and the microwave are concealed within the mezzanine staircase (only their doors are visible from the kitchen), and all the other kitchen appliances (washing machine, dishwasher, trash unit) are hidden within the white cabinets, so the overall effect is one of sleek uniformity.

ABOVE **By splitting the studio in two by means of the mezzanine staircase, the designers were able to give each part of the downstairs space a distinct identity without using walls.**

LEFT **With its integral desk and built-in lamps, Hills's office-meeting room needs no extra furniture and provides just the right amount of storage. All is concealed inside the floating unit, so the office does not intrude into the living space (INSET).**

OPPOSITE **The kitchen takes up almost half the apartment's floor area and feels light and spacious with its rows of white units, effective lighting, and semi-see-through furniture. The custom-built cabinets hold appliances, equipment, and general kitchen clutter so Hills can easily maintain a minimal look. The tiny bathroom, tucked inside the white corner cupboard (BELOW CENTER), is functional but unobtrusive.**

Built-in storage is one of the key ingredients of the successful small home because, tucked into the structure of a room, it doesn't intrude into the open space and thus makes the place feel bigger and less cluttered. Here, as we can see, it has been exploited to the full, not only in the kitchen and office but elsewhere, too. A series of white floor-to-ceiling cupboards, which constitute the side "wall" of the apartment, conceals vast amounts of clothes and clutter; further cupboards in the living "room" hide the music system, eliminating the usual mess of speakers and cables on the floor.

Because Hills had so much stuff to accommodate, the designers also included some more open storage space. In the kitchen, a stainless-steel rail, which is attached to the wall along the length of the units, houses baskets of flatware and utensils. Opposite, a shelving unit, the back of which cleverly forms the stairway wall, is filled with wine and tableware. Cantilevered off the floor (like the office units), this "floating" piece of furniture demonstrates another canny space-enhancing trick: leaving a gap between furniture and floor, so the flooring continues underneath, makes a space seem bigger.

Lighting (something photographer Hills was keen to get right) has also been used cleverly in this regard. Alongside the dimmable halogen spots that light the main space, tungsten tubes were tucked underneath the units and above the cupboards. While the fixtures are invisible, a warm glow emanates from the edges of the furniture—an effect that is particularly striking at night and suggests there is space beyond.

With its white walls and monochrome furnishings providing the perfect simple backdrop, this once one-dimensional space is now a fully functioning multipurpose home. Hills has space to work, sleep, eat, and entertain. "I often have 30 people dancing here," he admits. Lucky, then, that he has the pebble-like resin and marble floor. Hard-wearing and fantastically tactile, it was also right on brief. "What I really wanted," Hills explains, "was an urban beach house."

The kitchen (LEFT) was designed to take up the minimum of space while incorporating the maximum amount of built-in storage. The sleek white units conceal a washing machine and dishwasher, while the fridge and microwave are tucked into cupboards within the mezzanine staircase (ABOVE). A stainless-steel rail above the counter provides additional storage space for kitchen utensils (RIGHT).

FAR RIGHT **To free up wall space, Hills opted for low, cylindrical heaters rather than conventional wall-mounted radiators.**

# neat and
## narrow house

This tall, thin modernist house in London gives a brilliantly literal interpretation of living in a small space. Built on a site hardly big enough to swing a cat in and squeezed between buildings on either side, the place looks more mini office building than comfortable family home... and yet, the latter is just what it is. Behind its slender glass façade, the property boasts three bedrooms and three bathrooms; a kitchen, living room, and conservatory; a study, a laundry room, and a foyer. It's even got a roof terrace big enough to fit a table and chairs for four. All in all, plenty of room for owners Ben and Geraldine Atfield and their baby son, Thomas.

OPPOSITE AND BELOW RIGHT The living room on floor five might be small, but it doesn't compromise on comfort. Although the space is only 11½ feet (3.5m) wide, it seems far bigger and has plenty of room for all the requisite bits and pieces: two squashy leather sofas, a streamlined coffee table, even a wide-screen television. To give the impression of space, the architect's trick here was to keep the decoration of the room to a minimum (floors are stone; walls are white) and to keep all clutter out of sight (no trailing television cables or piles of videos, for example). The fact that the front wall is all window also makes the room seem without boundaries and far bigger than it really is, for the outdoor space feels like an extension of the interior.

ABOVE RIGHT The top floor of the house, which is half conservatory and half roof terrace, has spectacular views across the city. To highlight this, a fake window in the wood-paneled wall frames a section of the surrounding landscape.

From the outside it is hard to believe that such a tiny building could accommodate so much, but architect Jo Hagan designed the place ingeniously, making full use of the available space. Unable to extend the house laterally, he built upward instead, stacking seven small-scale levels one on top of the other. What he created, in essence, was a mini skyscraper (an apt conceit, given that the City of London's high-rises are just streets away) with as much internal space as your average row house—quite a feat on a plot of land just big enough for a London bus. It's 11½ feet (3.5m) wide by 33 feet (10m) deep, to be precise.

Exploiting space vertically rather than horizontally was a canny trick (and an economical one in a city where land comes at a premium), but it did pose new challenges, particularly when it came to planning the layout of the house. Whereas most homes allow an easy, same-level relationship between rooms used in connection with each other (the kitchen and the living room, for example), here lateral connection was impossible. Instead, each floor was given over to one living function (sleeping, say, or eating) and deciding which "room" should go where took on an altogether more crucial aspect. The Atfields, after all, didn't want to spend all their time traveling up and down between floors.

In the end, they reversed the usual formula of bedrooms at the top and living rooms at the bottom by placing the "public" spaces on the fifth and sixth floors. Here the façade of the building is glazed at both front and back, and not only fills the interior with light (there are no curtains or blinds) but also gives fantastic views over the city. It made sense, then, to use this area for the living room and conservatory (which leads onto the roof terrace), where they would entertain and spend most time. The bedrooms were positioned on the second and third floors where only the front façade is glazed (and can be curtained off for privacy) and where the darker back of the house could be used for bathrooms. The kitchen—the hub of the home—was placed in between (on floor four) to allow easy access from above and below.

The façade of the building is glazed at both front and back, and not only fills the interior with light but also gives fantastic views over the city.

Standing in these self-contained spaces with no views through to another room is an odd sensation, but surprisingly, the interior doesn't feel squashed or claustrophobic. This is largely thanks to that fully glazed façade, which—as well as turning the building into a mini modernist masterpiece—connects internal and external space so intimately. With wall-to-wall and floor-to-ceiling views at every level (bar the basement, of course), the house feels without boundaries, and the surrounding landscape becomes just an extension of the interior. This merging of indoor and outdoor space—typical of many a modernist home—visually tricks you into thinking the place is far bigger than it really is.

There are more prosaic reasons, too, why the interior feels spacious. Planning each floor of the house extremely tightly, Hagan made sure he used every bit of available space to the full. He built in wet-room bathrooms (no need for a shower cubicle) with integral shelving around the tub; he installed underfloor heating (no need for radiators); and— most important of all—he built in copious amounts of secret storage, making use of "dead" space that would otherwise have been wasted. At living room level, the hot water and heating paraphernalia are hidden under the stairs; in the bedrooms, capacious closets mark the entrance; in the bathrooms, mirrors conceal storage shelves. Even on the stairway, tucked at the back of the building to take up the least possible room, storage cupboards and lights are built into the walls.

ABOVE Taking up the least possible space at the back of the building is a narrow staircase, but the owners use it far less than the mini elevator that runs from first floor to top.

LEFT Tucked into a tiny space between existing buildings, this little house could be constructed in only one direction: up. Seven storys were stacked up to create the same amount of space that you would find in a conventional home. Unlike your average house, however, each floor accommodates just one room, with the public spaces—living room, conservatory, terrace—at the top, and the private—bedrooms and bathrooms—at the bottom. The kitchen is between the two on floor four for easy access (RIGHT). With its glazed façade, this mini skyscraper looks quite at home in its surroundings and, though it is the antithesis of most laterally biased living spaces, it functions very effectively as a family home.

conservatory and roof terrace

living room

kitchen

bedroom 2 and bathroom

bedroom 1 and bathroom

foyer laundry

basement bedroom 3 /study

section

LEFT  Ingeniously designed, the bathrooms don't feel as tiny as they really are. Built-in and wall-mounted fixtures free the central space, while secret storage areas allow clutter to be hidden from view. The integral shelf around the bathtub also provides a useful storage spot.

BELOW LEFT  Every bit of space in the building has been used to the full. Here, the entrance to the main bedroom has a large closet to accommodate clothes and clutter, thus freeing space in the room itself. Unlike the "public" areas upstairs, the bedrooms have floor-to-ceiling curtains so they can be screened from view.

With wall-to-wall and floor-to-ceiling views at every level, the house feels without boundaries, and the landscape becomes an extension of the interior.

The decoration of the house, too, does all it can to make the place feel expansive. White walls and simple stone flooring reflect the light; furniture is simple and streamlined; accessories are kept to a minimum. The result? A house that feels light, airy, and spacious, despite its diminutive dimensions, and one which works brilliantly as a contemporary home, even though it is the opposite of most laterally biased modern living spaces (think of all those urban lofts).

There is one element here that remains resolutely tiny, however: the elevator. A life-saver in a seven-story-high household, this little two-man car cuts a swathe from the first floor of the building right to the top and saves countless unnecessary journeys. "We use it as a dumb waiter," Ben Aftield laughs, "because it's more or less the same size."

ABOVE AND OPPOSITE  With its sleek white units, stone floors, and simple modern furniture, the kitchen seems bigger than most—an effect enhanced by the window wall at the front. Although there are no eye-level cupboards (avoided by the architect because they would have made the room seem more cramped), there is just enough storage space to accommodate all the kitchen clutter.

With a wraparound roof terrace on three sides, this New York apartment has fantastic views across the city—something designer David Khouri exploited to the full by creating a series of floor-to-ceiling glass doors around the perimeter of the property. They not only allow light to pour into the apartment from all sides, but also extend the sense of space, for the terrace itself—decorated with a pattern of tiled and planted paving and upholstered furniture—now feels very much part of the interior.

*(floor plan labels: living/dining area, bathroom, kitchen, study/guest bedroom, dressing area, bathroom, bedroom)*

# flexible space

Making the most of your space is one of those axioms of interior decorating that we all have in mind when we think about doing up our homes. Chanted by celebrity designers on television, analyzed by experts in the pages of interiors magazines, and demonstrated in a host of self-help design books, this little phrase is something we all know by heart. Few of us, however, have put it into practice as cleverly as the designer of this little apartment, perched on the 17th floor of a New York apartment building.

In a small space it is vital, of course, to make the most of every bit of it, something the previous owner of this property had singularly failed to do. Though the place wasn't sizeable (around 1,000 square feet or 93 square meters), it had fair credentials: a reasonable amount of floor space; windows on three sides; a sweep of roof terrace giving spectacular views over the south of the city. Nothing, however, had been done to fulfill this potential. The interior, for a start, was boxy and cramped, and extraordinarily, brick walls on all sides meant that there was little sight of the roof terrace (and thus those views) from inside.

The new owners of the apartment, Avi Pemper and Mark Rabiner, knew something had to be done, but rather than going down the conventional route and calling in an interior decorator, they asked

Comma designs are funky, colorful, and original (most of the furniture in the apartment is theirs)—just the qualities Pemper and Rabiner wanted for their new living space.

product designer David Khouri of Comma to undertake the project for them. "They came in to see our work and bought a screen," explains Khouri. "Things progressed from there." Though on the face of it, this might seem a rash decision, it is easy to see why the couple were won over. Comma designs are funky, colorful, and original (most of the furniture in the apartment is theirs)—just the qualities Pemper and Rabiner wanted for their new living space.

With faith in his design expertise, the couple gave a broad brief to Khouri. "They wanted to update the apartment and to turn it into somewhere that would keep them in the city at weekends," he explains. "They also wanted me to keep a bit of the building's original 1950s character." The first thing he did, of course, was to knock out the brick wall at the front of the building and replace it with floor-to-ceiling glass doors (reinforced in strategic places). This had an immediate and dramatic effect. Not only did light now pour into the interior, but the place instantly seemed more open and expansive, something that Khouri then enhanced by taking out the existing dropped plaster ceiling.

Once the structure of the interior had been rejigged, Khouri then set about rearranging the internal layout of the space. Rabiner and Pemper, like most contemporary couples, wanted an open-plan, do-it-all living area—somewhere they could eat, entertain, listen to music. They also wanted bathrooms, a kitchen, two bedrooms, a dressing room, a den, and an office. Rather than splitting the interior up into boxy rooms, however, Khouri decided instead to create flexible space. On one side of the apartment, he established a

THIS PAGE **On one side of the apartment is the living-dining room, which is filled with colorful and quirky furniture designed by Comma (except for the vintage sofa). The step up to the terrace (shown on page 25, below), topped with white vinyl cushions, can double as an ad hoc sitting area.**

OPPOSITE **A sleek, modern storage solution, the wall of cupboards hides everything from books and CDs to the hi-fi. Suspended off the floor and lit right around its perimeter, this unit and the polished stainless-steel box beside it seem less solid and thus don't diminish the overall sense of space.**

LEFT **Separated by sliding doors, the bedroom, dressing area, and office can be left open to each other to create one giant sleeping space or enclosed for privacy. The office (in the foreground of the main picture and inset) can also be turned into a spare bedroom, for the gray chairs (below) unfold to make a queen-size mattress.**

RIGHT **With plenty of storage in the two large units in the dressing area, the bedroom can be kept uncluttered. Though minimally furnished, it isn't stark. The grasscloth wallpaper and resin floor give textural interest.**

The rooms are separated by sliding partitions. "In a small space, it's nice not to have to deal with doors."

living-dining room (separating the two areas simply with that signature orange screen) and on the other, he constructed a series of three rooms—a master bedroom, a dressing room (just two storage units with a passage in between), and an office-den that can be turned, in an instant, into another bedroom.

Separated only by sliding partitions ("in a small space, it's nice not to have to deal with doors," says Khouri), these three rooms can be left open to each other to create one airy bedroom wing or enclosed to create private space—particularly useful when the couple have guests. Shut off from the dressing room, the office-bedroom with its little adjacent bathroom can thus be transformed into a self-contained suite.

The bathrooms and the kitchen could not be reworked structurally but Khouri did all he could decoratively to make the best of them. He mirrored the ceiling of the main bathroom to double the space visually and covered the walls of both in brilliantly reflective white structural glass. Unwilling to make do with average fixtures, Khouri had a bathtub and basin made out of white Corian (by Wilsonart Corporation) and supplemented them with custommade plastic and designer pieces (the long rectangular Cappellini sink in the master bathroom is one).

The kitchen, too, is the antithesis of average. Though it is a tiny space, it has bags of impact because of its ingenious and original design. All the surfaces are faced in a Corian-like material (white for the units and counter; orange for the sink), and the walls are lined with cupboards molded from self-skinning urethane (the stuff used to make dashboards). And that's not all. Hidden both above and beneath the cabinets are three different colors of neon, so that the room can change color at the flick of a switch ("the couple wanted party lighting," Khouri explains).

LEFT **Though tiny, the kitchen manages to be both funky and functional. With wraparound white units at floor level and molded urethane cupboards at eye level, there is plenty of storage. The appliances are built in, and the cooktop set into the counter makes the most of the space.**

RIGHT **The two bathrooms may be small, but they feel bright and spacious because of Khouri's clever use of materials. Walls are covered in reflective white structural glass; fixtures are white and in the main bathroom the ceiling is mirrored to double the space visually.**

## Hidden above the cabinets are three different colors of neon, so the kitchen can change color.

With his innovative designs and clever use of materials, Khouri has given the apartment a cool and individual stamp, but there is more to the place than mere designer looks; it is also full of pragmatic solutions for small-space living. For a start, the apartment is full of storage. The dressing room has two giant wood-veneered units; the bathrooms stacks of secret space for stashing bathing kit; the kitchen, units galore. And then there is the living "room" with its funky storage wall. Topped with rosewood and lined with red plastic laminate, it accommodates all manner of bits and pieces, and even houses a little bar at one end. Large and solid, this iconic piece could intrude on the rest of the space had Khouri not suspended it off the floor and sunk lighting around the perimeter to make it "float" (another natty space-saving trick).

Finally, there's the floor. A uniform plane throughout the apartment, it is made of glossy epoxy resin in a light cobalt blue. "We wanted it to look like a swimming pool," explains Khouri, "so we gave the manufacturer a color chip to match." In addition to being extremely hard-wearing, bringing all the disparate bits of the apartment together, and giving the place a hint of 1950s color, this shiny, highly reflective surface makes all the furniture seem to float (that swimming pool conceit worked like a dream) and fools the eye into thinking the apartment is far bigger than it really is. The original owner wouldn't recognize the place.

OPPOSITE AND RIGHT
Interior designer Helen Ellery let neither size nor location cramp her style when it came to doing up her diminutive London home. The living room looks more country cottage than urban row house and, though tiny, is filled with largish pieces of furniture. The expansive glass-topped cabinet and shelves hung in the alcoves beside the fireplace provide useful storage space.

# escape from the loft

Not many of us, I would hazard to guess, would choose to move from an expansive loft space into a teeny-weeny row house, but interior designer Helen Ellery did just that. She had had enough of that trendy open-plan lifestyle, of multipurpose living zones and all that undemarcated space. What she craved, instead, were some good old-fashioned rooms. "In a loft, you have just one big area to work with," she explains. "I wanted to have a number of different spaces so that I could stamp a distinctive personality onto each." She also wanted somewhere that would accommodate both her work and her living space without the one intruding on the other (something that is particularly tricky to achieve in a one-floor, open-plan loft).

This tiny little 1800s property on a quiet London street seemed, then, an unlikely place for Ellery to realize her ambitions. Though built on three floors, with a converted basement, the house is very small (the photographs are deceptive), and what's more, when she bought it, there

Ellery decided to use the basement and first floor (ABOVE) of the house for her office, keeping the top two floors for her home. On the second floor (LEFT) is the living room, dining room, and kitchen (with a roof terrace outside); on the third, two bedrooms and a tiny bathroom. The staircase is carpeted with a grass green runner—something which, along with other rugs in varying natural greens, helps to bring a touch of the countryside to this inner-city location.

were no rooms to speak of. The building had served a series of different functions over the centuries (hosiery store, tripe merchant, and salvage yard to name but three), and its original internal structure had been stripped out years previously. What Ellery inherited was, essentially, a shell, and a miniature one at that.

Ellery, however, saw the potential of the place and was particularly drawn by the fact that she could create a categoric split between her home and her office by placing them on different floors (her business, The Plot, now occupies the basement and first floor; her home, the top two floors). The size of the building also worked in Ellery's favor. Disenchanted with loft living, she wanted her new home to be more cozy country cottage than minimal urban penthouse. Diminutive dimensions were thus a bonus, even though space would be tight.

Having only a small area to work with, Ellery planned the layout of her home very carefully. On the lower floor, she needed to accommodate a living room, dining area, and kitchen (quite a challenge in such a restricted space). Rather than slicing the interior into three self-

contained rooms, Ellery created just one solid partition, a wall that runs across half the space and cleverly defines three separate areas. At the front of the house is the living room which, semi-enclosed by the central wall, feels private and cozy. Tucked behind the wall at the back of the house is the kitchen. In the space between, at the top of the stairs, is the tiny dining area, its perimeter defined only by a change of flooring and a giant stainless-steel fridge.

Although all three "rooms" are open to the others (a trick which, cleverly, makes them seem bigger than they really are), each has its own distinct identity. The living room is clubby and traditional with its chunky check sofa, large wooden cabinet, and raw brick fireplace.

ABOVE **Ellery's kitchen on the second floor doesn't feel at all cramped because it has been left open to both the dining and the living areas. To avoid these three "rooms" merging into each other decoratively, Ellery gave each a distinct identity. The kitchen is defined by a floor of black-and-white mini tiles and by a row of shiny black units that "almost disappear" when the sun shines on them. And Ellery has stacks of storage, from shelves and plate racks to hanging rails and hooks.**

2nd floor

3rd floor

kitchen

living room

bathroom

bedroom

bedroom

LEFT **Ellery has used every inch to turn a tiny two-story space into a fully functioning home. Upstairs, she extended the bedrooms up into the attic area to make them roomier and squeezed a mini bathroom onto the landing.**

LEFT **Although the house looks rustic and cozy with its tongue-and-groove paneling, chintzy colors, and comfy furniture, it is not a simple country cottage pastiche. Unconventional and quirky elements bring the interior to life and give it a contemporary, highly personal stamp. An upside-down cup and saucer becomes a quirky lampshade, for example, while a giant railway clock brings an *Alice in Wonderland* sense of scale to the dining area.**

The kitchen is rustic and chic, a combination of sleek black units ("almost invisible when the sun shines on them"), dark wood countertops, and rails of shiny steel utensils. The most striking feature here, however, is the floor, which has been covered with black-and-white mini tiles—a device that divides the kitchen visually from the dining area and also gives it a grandeur that belies its size. "It's a joke on those floors you find in stately homes," laughs Ellery. The dining "room"—the smallest of the three—comprises a simple wooden table and four chairs positioned underneath a giant old railroad clock.

Convention dictates that a small space should be furnished with small pieces of furniture, but Ellery has turned that on its head, filling her home with unexpectedly large-scale items: the giant fridge, the wall-to-wall living room cabinet, the oversized clock. "It's a myth that you can't use big things in small spaces," exclaims Ellery. "Furnishing with oversized objects—as long as they don't stop you from moving around freely—makes the atmosphere seem bigger." There is no doubt that these pieces appear to stretch the space around them; they also give a quirky *Alice*

Storage is the key to living successfully in any small space, and Ellery has incorporated a lot of it into her tiny home. In the guest bedroom (BELOW RIGHT), she placed the bed on a platform to create storage space underneath, while in the master bedroom (THIS PICTURE AND RIGHT), she installed a large built-in closet (in tongue-and-groove to match the walls) and a unit of open storage boxes to house her clothes. With its duck's-egg-blue walls, old-fashioned furniture, and floral curtains and valances, this room feels far removed from the urban landscape outside.

*in Wonderland* feel to the interior (the black-and-white miniature tiles do the same), which adds an extra, highly individual dimension.

Upstairs, too, Ellery used this little and large conceit. In her bedroom at the front of the house, the stripped sash windows are dressed with oversized valances and curtains in overblown floral fabric, which make the room feel larger than it is—a canny trick given that it's actually fairly small. Aside from one large built-in storage unit, there is only room for a bed (albeit a shapely, vintage, wooden one), a small side table, and an old working range, which was originally installed in the kitchen.

Fitting two bedrooms and a bathroom into the tiny upstairs floor was no easy feat, but Ellery made use of every available space. She took out the existing ceilings and extended the bedrooms up into what would have been the attic, giving them more room and also a more shapely, pitched outline. She then squeezed a narrow bathroom onto the landing which, otherwise, would have been wasted space—a good solution in any small house. Because

ABOVE AND RIGHT **Ellery used the "dead" space on the landing to accommodate this tiny bathroom, and even here she didn't compromise on style. She had grand, traditional fixtures made to fit, and she incorporated a built-in shelf beneath the mirror for her perennial displays of flowers. The towel rod was wall-mounted to free floor space.**

## Ellery's home is no country cottage pastiche. Off-beat touches bring the interior bang up to date.

the room is so tiny, Ellery had to get the fixtures specially made, but she didn't compromise on style (tank, basin, and shower kit are miniature versions of grand traditional pieces). There are other space-saving tricks at play here, too: the radiator (also a heated towel rod) is wall-hung to free up the floor, and an integral shelf has been built into the tiles to store bathroom clutter.

Storage, of course, is key in a space like this, and Ellery has plenty of it. The tiny spare bedroom has a platform bed (accessed by an old wooden ladder) with capacious cupboards underneath it. The main bedroom has a large closet and built-in alcoves for sweaters and shoes. In the living room, there is the long, glass-fronted cupboard; in the kitchen, old-fashioned plate racks, hanging rails, and shelves.

None of the above, however, feels intrusive, because Ellery's decorative scheme unifies every bit of the interior. Not only has she used a limited palette of soft country colors (duck's-egg blue and rich creams) throughout the house, she has also reinstated the tongue-and-groove paneling that would originally have lined the walls. Rather than making the place seem smaller—a result you might expect from such a linear feature—it looks completely at home and gives the interior cohesion and rustic charm.

Ellery's home is no country cottage pastiche, however: off-beat touches bring the interior bang up to date. There are the contemporary paintings by Robert Clarke, for example (floral, of course). There are the carpets, rugs, and runners in varying natural greens (rapeseed; country lawn; fields of wheat; and so on). There is the brown felt kitchen blind that looks for all the world like a roll of sod. And there is real nature, too. Vases and jugs filled with blossoms. Cedar windowboxes planted with wildflowers. The roof terrace covered with pots of plants and herbs. With outdoors as tangible as this, this dwelling feels rural and boundariless—quite an achievement for a teeny-weeny city row house.

By removing most of its internal walls, Jonathan Clark transformed a boxy and cramped interior into a spacious and flexible one. The bathrooms were tucked out of the way in the corridor along one side of the apartment; the bedroom and kitchen (BELOW RIGHT) placed at either end; and the biggest central space turned into a giant living-dining area (LEFT, RIGHT, AND FAR RIGHT). With natural light pouring in from three sides, this room is bright, gallery-like, and adaptable. Furnished simply with streamlined and modular pieces, such as a simple corner sofa and a sleek bench-shelf, it works both as a social space and as a more intimate family sitting room.

shower  bathroom

bedroom

living area

dining area/office/ guest bedroom

kitchen

# classic convertible

Now, as you know, this is a book about small spaces. So how can we, I hear you cry, include an apartment that is so palpably large? Well, the thing is, it's not; it just appears to be. At 925 square feet (86 square meters), this second-floor apartment is no bigger than a smallish basement flat, but with its high ceilings, ingenious layout, and clever design, it looks—of course—twice that size.

Home to Rashna Mody-Clark, art director of *House & Garden* UK, and architect Jonathan Clark, the place did not always seem so expansive. When they first bought it, the interior was a tangle of partitions and boxy rooms with one long, dark, curved corridor connecting the front of the house to the back. "It had been converted badly in the 1980s," explains Clark, "and it was a very divided space. Rashna hated it." Clark, however—drawn by the height and by the volume of the place—knew he could do something with it.

The property had other noticeable assets, too. For a start, it was end of row, which meant natural light could pour in on three sides. And then there was the fact that it borrowed space from the next-door building. Not only is the communal staircase situated in the adjacent house,

The dining area (see plan on previous page) can be sectioned off behind an ingenious sliding partition (LEFT) to create an extra, enclosed room. When not in use, this ceiling-hung divider folds away unobtrusively into the architecture of the interior; when in use, it is as solid and soundproof as a proper wall. Decorated simply and flexibly, this extra room can swap roles seamlessly and can change from dining area to private guest bedroom to quiet home office with the minimum of fuss. On one side, the room is lined with white floor-to-ceiling cupboards that accommodate all the necessary kit (a folding bed and bedding, for example) and which also conceal the mini work station (RIGHT). When the room is not shut off, however, it simply becomes an extension of the main living place (OPPOSITE), and home to a long and sleek dining table and chairs (INSET).

but—bizarrely—the kitchen is, too (although not obvious inside the apartment, on the plan it is easy to see that the room extends through the party wall). Whatever the reason for this unusual layout, it meant that there was a reasonable amount of unadulterated space for Clark to play with.

Once he had stripped out all the unnecessary partitions (and there were many), Clark's first plan was to turn what had been a poky three-bedroom flat into a capacious and open one-bedroom apartment. A local realtor advised him, however, that this would be a foolish move, making the place harder to sell in the future, so Clark, instead, came up with the idea of creating multipurpose space. Using the large, light area at the front of the house for a living room and keeping the main bedroom at the back, he converted what had been the second bedroom in the center of the apartment into a dining room-office-guest room.

Multipurpose rooms provide an ingenious solution to the shortage of space problem as long as they can perform each function required of them effectively and as long as one role doesn't submerge the others (it's no good, for example, combining an office and a guest room if you allow business clutter to swamp the latter). Here the central zone is neutral enough to be very adaptable, and on account of its ingenious design, it can easily play one role (as dining room, say) without evidence of the others intruding.

In dining mode, this flexible space has all the requisite pieces: table; chairs; floor-to-ceiling cupboards; and a decorative walnut panel on the wall in place of a painting. It is open to the living

The central zone is neutral enough to be very adaptable, and on account of its ingenious design, it can easily play one role without evidence of the others intruding.

Clark has made clever use of frosted glass partitions to screen private areas while bringing light into the central space. Here a floor-to-ceiling glass panel hides the shower room from view, while a shorter frosted screen encloses the corner of the sitting area, separating it from the bathroom corridor, but leaving a narrow window to allow a view through the apartment.

## Mosaic-tiled bathing spaces make brilliant use of a narrow strip of space on one side.

area, creating one large L-shaped room that is brilliant for entertaining. When guests come to stay, however, everything changes. A folding bed comes out of the cupboards; the wooden panel becomes a headboard; table and chairs are moved into the living area and—best of all—the room is completely enclosed behind a sliding acoustic wall (an idea that Clark picked up from a conference hall). This substantial, three-paneled device, stacked neatly away into an alcove when not in use, is hung from tracks in the ceiling and creates a solid, soundproof barrier when extended. The soundproofing is also very useful when Rashna wants to use the room as an office (her business and computer equipment is, like the bed, cleverly concealed in one of the capacious white cupboards).

Building flexibility into an interior is a forte of Clark's, and convertible design is evident

**By placing the bathroom and shower room end to end at one side of the apartment, Clark maximized space for the central living area. Enclosed behind sliding doors (far more space-saving than hinged ones) or simply left open to the corridor, these tiny utility spaces take up little room but are highly functional. Storage space, for example, is hidden beneath the colorful mosaic countertops.**

everywhere you turn in this apartment. The main bedroom and bathroom at the back of the house, for example, can be closed off from the rest of the space by means of a pivoting door (something that is particularly key for privacy as the bathtub is open to view from the corridor). The shower room, too, can be concealed behind a sliding door or left open to the main space to increase the light.

These twin mosaic-tiled bathing spaces make brilliant use of a narrow strip of space on one side of the apartment (something that Clark couldn't change because of three immovable service pipes that were installed in the 1980s). Though you might expect any corridor-based room to be dark and poky, these are quite the reverse. Placed end-to-end and fitted with sliding doors and frosted glass and mirrors in strategic places, they seem spacious and are filled with light. "You have

LEFT **Chic and hotel-like, the master bathroom (beside the bedroom) has been left partially open to the corridor. This not only extends the boundaries of the room, making it feel bigger, but also provides an intimate connection to the bedroom. Although doors are not Clark's favorite feature, he did make a concession here, installing a swing door between this bathroom and the rest of the apartment. When it is open, there is a view across the main space from front to back, but when it's shut, bedroom and bathroom are private.**

to make the best you can of daylight," says Clark, whose use, here, of frosted glass panels to divide space (most noticeably between the shower room and the living area) maximizes any natural light there is.

The result of Clark's reworking of the apartment's interior is dramatic. The place feels huge because you can see (when the doors are open, that is) right across it from all sides and also because the windows and vertical planes of architecture take the eye right up to those high ceilings. It is not only the structure of the thing, however, that makes the interior seem spacious; it is also the fact that it is simply furnished and fairly empty. Aside from a few well-chosen bits of mid-century furniture, a sofa that makes a perfect fit around one corner of the living room ("I designed the walls around it," laughs Clark) and a few built-in pieces, there is little else. No boxes, no books (on show, at least): no clutter.

The reason for this? That good old space-saver, storage, something there is stacks of in this interior. In addition to the floor-to-ceiling cupboards in the dining-guest room and the streamlined custommade cabinet in the living room, Clark provided a huge amount of less visible storage space. In the bedroom, for example, the sleek wood-paneled wall is all cupboards; in the bathrooms, the blue mosaic hides space for

## There is a huge amount of less visible storage. In the bedroom the sleek wood-paneled wall is all cupboards.

stashing bathroom things. Most dramatic of all, however, are the two storage "platforms" that Clark created to make the most of the high ceilings. With one running between the dining room and bathrooms and the other from the bedroom above the newly created walk-in closet (previously bedroom number three), these mezzaninelike storage spaces are big enough to sleep on and house everything from the heating system to a library of old magazines.

"It is rare, particularly in cities, to be able to build new," comments Clark. "You tend to have to mess around with an existing structure, and I always try to make an interior seem bigger than it really is. You have to make the most of what you have." With every inch of space exploited to the maximum, there is no doubt that here he has done just that.

ABOVE AND RIGHT **Encased in black walnut, the bedroom is the height of contemporary chic, but none the less practical for that. The wooden wall behind the bed, which stretches to the ceiling, conceals stacks of storage. Though the sleek façade is marked out in regular squares, the cupboards come in various sizes: one square for small things, several for the wardrobe. Boxing in the head of the bed meant Clark could use the cupboard sides for bedside lights. The window, with its pull-up blind to give privacy without shutting out the sky, acts as a headboard.**

# **manhattan** miniature

**Planning the layout of a small space is like doing a
complicated 3-D jigsaw puzzle and can seem just as
impossible a task at the outset. You need to fit in all the
requisite rooms… and you only have 650 square feet
(60 square meters) to do it in. Where do you start? This
was the challenge facing New York designer Shamir Shah
when he embarked on the renovation of this tiny apartment
on the parlor floor of a classic Manhattan brownstone.**

When he first saw the property, it was a mess. The kitchen and
bathroom fixtures were "horribly dull"; ceilings were low and space was
cramped. "I wanted to make it clean, comfortable, and uncluttered,"
explains Shah. Given the size of the place, he had his work cut out.

Shah, however, wasn't daunted. He has made a name for himself
designing chic hotels and shops (including one for internationally acclaimed
potter Jonathan Adler), and he recently created a loft for Ian Schrager,
the man behind a string of hip hotels. Reconfiguring this space was a
challenge, but one Shah was ready for. "Working small spaces takes more
thought and careful planning," he says, "but it's also extremely rewarding."

His first task was to gut the place and then to change its structure so
every bit of the space could be used to its full potential. He removed the
existing false ceiling and reinstated the house's original 12-foot (4-meter)
one; he made the doorways taller and put in long vertical casement
windows that would draw attention to the height of the space. He then

Half of the main living area acts as both dining space and home office. The walls are lined with custommade mahogany cupboards (not shown) and shelves that carry everything from books and pictures to the refrigerator. The dining table-desk slots neatly under the bottom shelf to save space.

living room

bedroom

study

bathroom

kitchen

Dark wood contributes to the beautiful diffused light of the dining and working area.

rejigged the layout of the apartment, creating a small entry hall (see page 47), which allowed him to separate the bedroom on the other side and also to incorporate a wall of storage.

Most of the apartment's floor area was then given over to a multipurpose living, dining, and working room, with a sitting area at the front (by the windows) and an office-eating area at the back. These two different "zones" are separated only by a neat wooden desk/dining table, which juts out across the room in the center, so—kept more or less open-plan—

ABOVE Shah reconfigured the interior to give most space to the area where he spends most time.

RIGHT Often in a small home, rooms are kept minimally furnished and surfaces uncluttered to make them seem bigger than they really are. Here, however, the owner chose to fill his space with a personal mix of furniture and objects that give it a good dose of comfort and character. The look—sort of 1940s French meets tribal—is unfussy, however, and the furniture streamlined and elegant, so the room does not seem cramped or overwhelmed.

The entire place—
even the bathroom
—is wired for sound
("a must in any small
space," urges Shah).

part of the overall storage scheme, housing everything from stereo equipment, books, and files to the linen cupboard and even the fridge. "It's the best use of space in the whole apartment," says Shah, largely because it means that surfaces throughout can be kept clean and uncluttered. The fact that the entire place—even the bathroom—was also wired for sound ("a must in any small space," urges Shah) makes the minimal look that much easier to achieve, of course.

Elsewhere, there is more storage space. In the bedroom, a large floor-to-ceiling closet and a custommade mahogany chest of drawers accommodate copious amounts of clothes and clutter; in the hall, a tall, thin closet houses coats and, more surprisingly, the catbox (hence the cutout square at the bottom of the door). "Putting it here seemed the obvious solution to me," explains Shah, "but it has raised an eyebrow or two!"

More unusual, however, are the size and location of the kitchen and bathroom. Squeezed side by side into a minuscule space at the back of the apartment, these two functional rooms are so small you hardly realize they are there at all. Now, while this layout might not suit an avid cook or a sybarite, it proved the ideal solution here. By sacrificing space in the utility areas, Shah was able to give a sense of scale to the main living spaces—the bedroom, the living room, and the dining room-office. The result? A compact apartment that doesn't feel squashed or claustrophobic, but quite the reverse. "It is a very functional, comfortable place," says Shah. "It never feels horribly cramped for space."

each seems to gain space from the other. Though the areas are two parts of the same room, they have distinct identities because Shah has decorated them very differently. The sitting area is all neutral colors and soft furnishings; the dining and working area dark and geometric, its walls lined with storage units in rich mahogany.

Opting for such a dark wood in such a small space is unusual (received decorating wisdom tells us that light colors make a room look bigger), but Shah is unrepentant. "Dark wood works better with my designs," he explains, adding that it also contributes to the beautiful diffused light of the space. Using such contrasting tones is also a clever way of dividing up the room visually, leading the eye from the functional eating area to the soft and pale "relaxing" area beyond. What's more, although both bits of the room are more or less the same size, the color change does indeed make the latter look larger.

The dark mahogany cupboards—which line the dining area walls like kitchen units—do more than provide contrast, however. Designed by Shah (like most of the furniture in the apartment), they are an integral

ABOVE Squeezed into the tiniest space possible, the fitted kitchen couldn't be more compact.

FAR LEFT, CENTER, AND LEFT Even in the small bedroom, which leads off the main space, there is room for modern and tribal art. There is also storage, with a wall of cupboards on one side and a chest of drawers (with space for books at the bottom) by the bed. The television is wall mounted to free floor space; a tall mirror makes the room feel bigger still.

OPPOSITE **This ingenious storage system in the living-dining area houses books, CDs, and general clutter. The doors—covered in Alpi veneer—flap either up or down for maximum flexibility.**

LEFT **Built in the late 1960s and early 1970s, London's fiercely modern Barbican comprises around 2,000 apartments.**

RIGHT **By stripping out internal walls, Daly opened up the interior, making it lighter and more spacious. Strategically placed mirrors also increase the sense of space.**

BELOW **By using panels of color, Daly made both walls and furniture appear less solid—a trick that helps make the space seem less confined.**

# high-rise bachelor pad

When it was first built in the late 1960s and early 1970s, the Barbican—London's experimental housing and cultural development—was in the hinterland of the financial heart of the city. For most, it seemed an inhospitable place in an inhospitable location. How times have changed. Today, the Barbican is at the epicenter of fashionable London, with trendy Clerkenwell to the west and even trendier Hoxton just a skip away to the east. It's become one of the city's hottest properties; an aspirational address if ever there was one.

There is, however, still a problem. The Barbican apartments (and there are around 2,000 of them) are—like many such purpose-built properties—jolly small (apart from the most expensive penthouses, that is). The originals have all the necessary accouterments (bedroom, bathroom, kitchen, living room); they may even have a view; but most also have gloomy and boxy 1960s interiors that do the location no favors. This apartment, owned by credit analyst Yuen-Wei Chew,

RIGHT Custom-built for the interior, the modular storage system is both highly functional and very funky. It "floats" off the floor to give the impression of continuing space underneath—a good way of making an interior seem larger.

LEFT An integral wooden desk, built as part of the storage system, is used as a mini home office whenever necessary. The seat, which doubles up as a dining chair, slots neatly underneath.

was no exception. Constructed in an L-shape with tiny rooms running off a long, dark corridor, it wasn't really the sleek, modern pied-à-terre he was hoping for. "It was a tiny space and very boring," Chew explains. "I knew I had to get someone to sort it out for me."

You can see from the pictures that he did just that, commissioning designer Paul Daly to transform the place into the ultimate urban bachelor pad. On the face of it, Daly was an unexpected choice. Although renowned for his nightclub and restaurant work, he had never designed a domestic interior before. Chew, however, was drawn by his ideas and his creative energy. "He had made restaurant spaces look very exciting with his imaginative use of light and materials," he says by way of explanation. "I hoped he could do the same here."

Daly's first move was to make the most of the available space by opening up the interior as much as he could. He stripped out the walls that surrounded the kitchen to make it part of the main living area (it had previously been completely enclosed but for a serving hatch). He knocked through the toilet and bathroom to make one reasonable-sized room—now done out top-to-toe in funky two-tone rubber. And he removed most of the internal doors (there were three just between the bedroom and the kitchen). "Getting the layout right was the key to everything," says Daly. "I wanted to create somewhere I could wander through."

His reworking of the structure of the interior made an enormous difference to the apartment. Now space flows freely between all areas and, wherever you stand, there are glimpses of rooms beyond (a good space-extending trick). Also, by removing the barriers between the front and the back of the apartment, Daly created a view right through the space, from the main living room

**BELOW AND RIGHT Now** open to the main living space, the kitchen is light and colorful. Given definition by a change of flooring and by the large overhead lighting panel, it is compact but also highly efficient. All the appliances are concealed behind closed doors, and an island unit, put on castors so it can be wheeled to one side, provides counter and storage space.

With its camouflagelike veneer and preponderance of browns and tans, the decoration seems more funky Pop than Zen, though there are some Eastern touches.

BELOW **The bathroom is the only enclosed room, so Daly gave himself free rein with its decoration. Unlike the stylish masculine look of the rest of the** apartment, this room is pure 1970s with its rounded corners and orange and beige rubber interior. "It looks as if it's been beamed in," he laughs.

window to the bedroom window, which not only makes the outside very much part of the interior, but also allows light to flood inside.

Daly didn't stop at structural changes, however. Wanting to enhance the feeling of openness he had created with an uncluttered, relaxing interior, he dictated every aspect of the decoration from the flooring right down to the paintings on the walls. His inspirations, he says, were healing spaces and the East, and his plan, to encourage Chew to eliminate clutter and pare down his possessions. "His taste is very eclectic," explains Daly. "There was loads of different stuff thrown together and no cohesion. We urged him to get rid of it all."

Chew, eager to simplify his life and lead that minimal modern existence, was compliant, partly—perhaps—because he knew that the decluttering task would be relatively easy given the enormous amount of built-in storage constructed by Daly. In the main living space, there is a "bookshelf" that combines dark wood shelves with box units covered in decorative Alpi veneer. Attached with magnets and hinges, the front of each box swings both up and down so you can easily change the dynamics of the piece, and what's more, you can open the doors with one hand.

The most impressive storage solution, however, comes in the form of the giant walk-in closet in the bedroom—inspired by a huge filing cabinet that Daly spotted at an exhibition. Made of Jacobean stained oak, with a panel of veneer and an integral mirror, this piece accommodates Chew's vast

A play of geometric shapes, the bedroom contains all the requisite features—bed, closet, mirror—in a smart, tightly designed configuration. The bed floats off the floor to suggest space beneath, while the panel of Alpi veneer provides a visual link to the living room.

collection of suits as well as copious amounts of other clothes and clutter. Doubling up as the bedroom "wall" on one side, it also stands as an iconic piece of furniture in its own right.

With its camouflagelike veneer and preponderance of browns and tans, the decoration seems more funky Pop than Zen, though there are some Eastern touches: the raked-sand effect flooring, for example; the mesmeric circular paintings on the walls (by Carol Robertson); the simplicity of the furnishing. Much of the scheme, however, was designed with a more pragmatic goal in mind: to make the space look bigger than it really is.

One canny device was to paint the walls with panels of color, leaving areas of plaster exposed. Daly did this partly to show off the "beautiful, uneven" plaster, but by painting

The bedroom area was built around Chew's vast collection of clothes, which needed suitable storage. Daly's solution was an ingenious double closet, made of two vast wooden units. Though the back one is fixed, the front unit, which also forms the bedroom wall (ABOVE), is on a track so it can be pulled farther into the bedroom (RIGHT), giving Chew access to his clothes, or pushed right up against the other unit to form an iconic block. Inside, the space is customized with hanging rods and shelves for all Chew's bits and pieces (FAR RIGHT).

only in sections, he also managed to make the walls seem less solid and the perimeter of the apartment thus more diffuse. He also made some of the furniture "float" by leaving a gap between the bottom of a piece and the floor (again, a good way of blurring boundaries and extending the perception of space). The bed, for example, was custom-built with a shadow gap around the base.

And then, of course, there is the lighting—something that Daly, as a nightclub designer, is an expert at. So often overlooked in contemporary interiors, a clever scheme can make a dramatic impact, particularly in a small, open-plan space that might otherwise lack differentiation. Here, as well as illuminating the

Doubling up as the bedroom "wall" on one side, the closet also stands as an iconic piece of furniture in its own right.

main living space of the apartment with cutting-edge multidirectional lamps, Daly used other light features to define different areas. What remains of the original corridor, for example, is transformed with two luminescent blue lightboxes; the kitchen has three separate settings so that at night it can be given an otherworldly purple glow. "I didn't want it to look just like a redundant utility space when it wasn't in use," explains Daly—an understandable concern, given that it is now so much part of the main living area.

The result of Daly's work is impressive. Although just like its neighbors outside, Chew's tiny apartment couldn't be more different within. Spacious, uncluttered, and very funky (all those nightclubby lights), it's just the sleek, modern pied-à-terre he had in mind.

# paris match

In the pictures, this Paris apartment looks fairly sizeable. It's got a sitting area with a large squashy sofa. It's got a space for dining. It's got the requisite utility rooms: kitchen, bathroom, bedroom. It also has a work station and copious amounts of storage. In reality, however, this is a tiny space. Measuring just 500 square feet (46 square meters), it is also a highly unusual triangular shape: not the ideal ingredients for a comfortable contemporary home.

Architects Fabienne Couvert and Guillaume Terver took on the challenge of creating one, however, even though when they first saw the place, it was very unprepossessing. Cramped and dingy, the interior had been carved up into three small rooms—a fact that did nothing to capitalize on the apartment's only asset: a series of six windows that run along the wall at the front of the property.

When they set to work on the place, the first thing Couvert and Terver did was to remove all the internal partitions, to open up the space, and to expose those windows. They then had a harder task, however—to reconfigure the interior so that it could accommodate all the necessary "rooms" without compartmentalizing it and blocking out the light.

The scheme they devised was simple but ingenious. They decided to divide the space simply by using two giant units, placed slightly apart in the middle of the apartment. Running parallel to the longest wall, they mark a separation between a row of utility rooms at the back and a living area at the front. Like vast screens, they partition space without confining it and help to delineate the different zones of the interior.

To create a coherent and open interior within this small triangular apartment, the architects constructed two giant units that divide space without confining it (RIGHT). The bedroom, bathroom, and toilet are tucked behind these along the back wall of the apartment, freeing space at the front for a large living-dining area. Flooded with light from the six windows and with a view across the space from the dining zone (OPPOSITE) to the lounging zone (LEFT), this area feels much bigger than it is.

*Floor plan labels:* kitchen · bathroom · bedroom · dining area · living area

When you enter the apartment, the first room you come to is the kitchen, which, together with the small eating area, fills one corner of the triangle. Extending into the main living space, with its perimeter defined by the dining table, the kitchen feels like a room, even though the working part of it—the units and appliances—is contained simply along the back wall under a thick ash countertop. Compact and cleverly designed, the kitchen and dining area can also act as office space out

of cooking and eating hours. The table becomes a desk, and the white floor-to-ceiling units open up to reveal a mini work station complete with boxes of files.

The back of the kitchen is screened from the main space by the first of the giant freestanding units, which not only acts as the

THIS PAGE **The dining area forms part of the kitchen, which runs along the back wall. A simple row of streamlined units, this is as compact as it gets, yet a mini office has been squeezed into one of the cupboards** (ABOVE RIGHT).

THIS PICTURE AND BELOW LEFT
**The two giant room dividers also provide stacks of much-needed storage. The first acts as an extra kitchen wall and is fitted with modular metal shelves, housing everything from glasses and tableware to boxes of provisions. The second (with a yellow interior), which screens the bathroom from view, has a low wooden bench-shelf with storage space underneath. This unit has also been topped with a screen of glass, which goes right up to the ceiling to increase the sense of privacy.**

kitchen wall, but also, fitted with a series of metal shelves and boxes, provides abundant flexible storage space. The second unit which, unlike the first, has been extended right up to the ceiling with a panel of glass, conceals the bathroom. This little mosaic-tiled room, effectively built in a corridor, has sliding doors at each end so it can be turned into a self-contained area when in use. Although you might expect such a tiny, enclosed space to be dark or cramped, it is neither. Light from the front windows pours through the glass extension, and mirrors, mounted to the back of the dividing unit, make the most of it.

OPPOSITE **Along the back wall of the apartment, a modular metal shelving system accommodates books, files, and pictures. While most of the shelves are left open, some have solid ash boxes that open like drawers and contain more personal possessions. This wall of storage extends into the adjoining bedroom** (LEFT).

RIGHT **The tiny bathroom can be enclosed at both ends by sliding doors. On one side is a wet-room area with a shower and a tiny wall-mounted basin. The other bathroom wall—the back of the second giant unit—is equipped with a mirror and cabinet.**

Beyond the bathroom, at the other end of the corridor, sits the bedroom. Partially hidden from the living area by an ash screen (placed directly alongside the second unit), this room—like the kitchen—is half-open and half-contained, making it private but not claustrophobic. With little space for furniture, the bedroom contains just a simple bed and a modular storage system that runs through the bedroom opening and right across the back wall of the apartment. Here, topped with books, alarm clock, and lamp, it acts as bedside table; in the adjacent living room, it holds everything from books and magazines to files and sweaters, allowing surfaces elsewhere to be kept clutter-free.

And so to this sitting-dining area. Running right across the apartment, and with its wall of windows, this space feels expansive and open— quite a feat in such a tiny place. Long diaphanous curtains, which give a good dose of color and fluidity to what would otherwise be a monochrome and very structured space, accentuate this home's airiness and give it a grandeur that, in its new configuration, it well deserves.

the zones

The key to living in any small space is to keep it as uncluttered and unfussy as you can. The owners of this room have filled it with streamlined pieces of furniture and used a very understated decorative scheme to make it feel as spacious as possible.

# living space

The place where most of us spend most of the time, the living room tends to be one of the biggest areas in a home. How often have you seen a kitchen squeezed into a corner, a dining room knocked out of existence, or a side return eaten up into an interior just to make way for a large, spacious living area? It is easy to see why this part of the home demands so much space today. Where once the living (or drawing or sitting) room was used simply for relaxing and entertaining—a space apart from the hustle and bustle of the dining room and kitchen—over the past twenty years, particularly, it has taken on a vast number of new roles. It is where we unwind; where we chat with our friends; where we watch television; where we listen to music. It may also be where we work and where we eat. As our homes have become more informal and less divided places, the living room has become the ultimate multipurpose space.

It would be easy for those of us with small homes to be put off by all those giant do-it-all living areas we see in glossy magazines and to think that we simply haven't the space to create something similar in our own interiors. We should not be deterred, however. The fact that homes are no longer expected to contain a series of single-function rooms and,

instead, can contain doubled- or even tripled-up areas (the kitchen-dining-sitting room, for example) can only be a blessing for those of us with little space. We may not have a basement to convert; we may not have a dining room to knock through; but we can still create a multifunctional living area in miniature.

Of course, the more roles a room will play, the more you will need to fit into it, so tight planning and clever design are particularly crucial in a small space. In this section, I will cover the key problem areas for the living room (how to accommodate all that audiovisual kit, for example) but for more general space-saving ideas, look to the Solutions chapter.

One last thing: if you have a small self-contained living room and love it, keep it. You don't have to follow the contemporary grain by opening everything up, and there is much to be said for the diminutive cottage look (see pages 32–37). There are also many ways you can make even a tiny, enclosed space seem bigger (if you want to). Read on.

## INCREASING SPACE: STRUCTURAL SOLUTIONS

If you need more space and have a reasonable budget to work with, think first about what changes you can make to the structure of your home. Major building projects, such as extensions, for example, will cost a lot of money, but there may be less drastic alterations you can make. Can you knock two rooms together (a front room and hall, perhaps) to create one larger living area? Do you have false ceilings that

ABOVE **Creating built-in storage spaces, such as this open wall unit, is often the best solution in a small room. Painted the same color as the surrounding walls, it is functional without being obtrusive.**

RIGHT **The owners of this property took a radical approach to increase their space. They completely removed the existing low ceilings to give themselves a bright, double-height living area.**

**LEFT** By opening up the ground floor of his tiny row house, garden designer Stephen Woodhams created a view right through the downstairs space from front to back. Because the eye is immediately drawn away from the entrance corridor and toward the open dining room and yard beyond, the place feels less confined than it is.

**BELOW LEFT** Simple, geometric, and modern, this built-in fireplace is far less fussy than a more traditional model and also incorporates neat alcoves above.

could be removed to give you more height (see page 45)? Could you incorporate the kitchen into the corner of the main living space and thus give yourself an extra room to work with? Seek advice from an architect or structural engineer before you start removing walls, but be open to the possibility of manipulating the bare bones of your home. It could make all the difference.

Consider smaller-scale structural changes, too. Even minor alterations, such as repositioning a door, can have an unexpectedly major impact. This may sound obvious, but it is something few of us think about: if a door opens into a room, it eats up a fair bit of space in the process. The solution? Simply rehang it so that it opens the

## Simplify the fireplace by removing the mantelpiece to create a plain, geometric hole in the wall.

other way. Alternatively, you could substitute sliding doors for swing versions or—if you're into open-plan living—eliminate the things altogether. Just think of the space you'll save. By doing away with doors, you may also be able to create a view right through your interior from front to back: a great visual trick that cons the eye into thinking that there is more space than there really is.

### SPACE-SAVING HEATING

Whether you have a traditional fireplace, ugly horizontal radiators, or both, heating paraphernalia takes up a lot of wall space—something you have all too little of in a small room. Add to this the fact that you can't, generally, put anything in front of a heat source and your scope for furnishing becomes increasingly limited. What can be done?

Well, the ideal solution is to get rid of the equipment altogether by installing underfloor heating, but this is not always a possibility. For a start it can cost a lot of money (though less so if you are building from scratch and don't have to take out an existing radiator system). What's more, underfloor heating isn't suitable for all living spaces and all kinds of floor covering (check before you commit to anything). The pipes and insulation that have to be laid beneath the floor also take up a fair amount of space—3in (8cm) or so—so if yours is a very shallow room, this may not be the best solution for you.

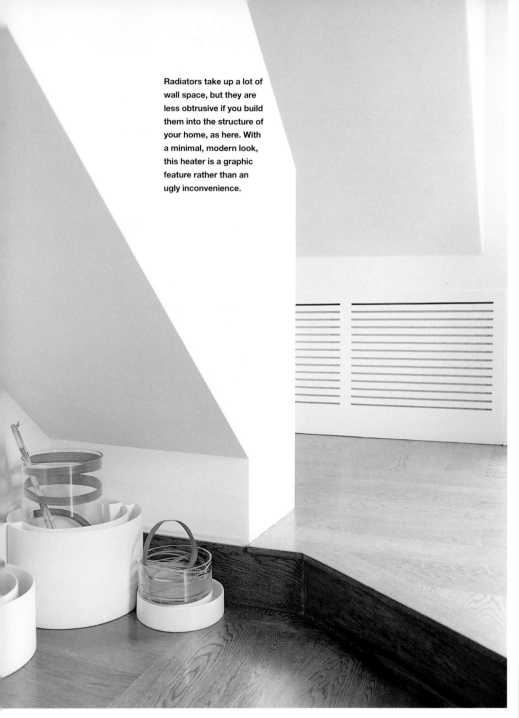

Radiators take up a lot of wall space, but they are less obtrusive if you build them into the structure of your home, as here. With a minimal, modern look, this heater is a graphic feature rather than an ugly inconvenience.

along the base of a wall or, better still, be sunk into a gully; a small wood-burning stove (which will give out lots of heat) can be placed in the center of a room or even against a window, giving you maximum flexibility elsewhere.

Solutions for fireplaces can be just as dramatic. If you are very short of space, why not take out the chimney (but note that the stack will need to be supported, so again, consult a structural engineer) and use it as a storage cupboard or bookshelves? Alternatively, just simplify the fireplace by removing the mantelpiece to create a plain, geometric hole in the wall. This modern solution will retain a focal point for the room (always useful), use less space, and make the interior less cluttered visually.

Consider other simpler options, such as moving a radiator into a dead space (under a window, for example) or invest in space-saving heating kit. There are many products on the market designed specifically for small areas, so see which works best for you. A tall, thin vertical radiator will free up lateral wall space and, even better, draw the eye up, increasing the sense of height; low industrial-style spiral heaters can run

RIGHT **Setting heating equipment back from the wall by fitting it into an alcove, as here, is also a good way of freeing space on all sides. It's neater visually, too.**

THIS PAGE In this pared-down apartment, the audiovisual equipment has been cleverly hidden behind a sleek panel of wood that looks more like modern art than anything functional. CDs, too, have been tucked out of sight inside a long horizontal box, which is attached to the wall like a Donald Judd installation.

## HOW TO HIDE YOUR HI-FI

What to do with an increasing amount of audiovisual gear is a perennial problem for any home owner, but it takes on more resonance in a tiny living room. What you don't want is a collection of mismatched units stacked up in a corner with cables trailing; what you should be after, instead, is an ordered or, better still, a concealed system, which will reduce clutter and thus make your room seem bigger.

If you are completely restructuring your living room, try to get as many of the brown goods as you can built in. DVDs, stereos, videos, speakers, and even the television can be hidden in a cupboard built just for the purpose (see pages 10–17). Television cabinets may have had a bad press in the past, but the concept of concealment was a good one. It works especially well if you create not individual storage units for each item but a seamless wall of floor-to-ceiling cupboards that can accommodate all of them and more (this way, when the doors are closed, the

## TOO MANY BOOKS

Books take up huge amounts of space, and if you want to keep a collection, you will need to create an effective storage system. Hide them, if you can, in built-in cupboards, or create a shelving system (though books on show will clutter up your room visually). If you have no space for cupboards or shelves, install a long low benchlike plinth along a wall and hide your books underneath or keep most of your collection stored away (in the attic, perhaps) and just stack up your favorites on the floor like a coffee table (see page 52).

*For space-saving furniture ideas, see page 132.*

cupboards become almost invisible). If you can't afford to build new storage, make the most of what you have and think laterally. Place the television in that revamped fireplace —as long as the fireplace is not still in use— or put it on a pivoting arm and attach it to the wall or in an unused alcove. If money is no object, you could always buy yourself an almost flat plasma-screen television, of course, and hang it, like a painting, on the wall.

ABOVE **With a sleek flat-screen plasma television mounted on the wall, the interior is free of bulky boxes and trailing cables.**

RIGHT **Even if you can't stretch to sleek units for your books and CDs, make sure to stack them up neatly. A bit of order makes the tiniest home seem more spacious.**

# SPACE SAVERS
## FOR **LIVING ROOMS**

★ Create a floor-to-ceiling wall of storage. It won't intrude on your space, and it should house a great deal of clutter.

★ Hide away your audiovisual kit and, if possible, conceal cables under floorboards or in the baseboard.

★ Get your speakers built in so they don't clutter up the main floor area.

★ Create a heating system that works with your space rather than against it. Treat yourself to "invisible" underfloor heating if you can.

★ Reverse the position of your door if it is taking up too much space.

★ If you don't want a fireplace, use the chimneybreast for shelving or storage.

★ If you do, simplify the fireplace and keep your mantelpiece neat.

★ In a shallow space, keep the seating low: floor cushions are de rigueur in stylish households.

★ Invest in furniture that does two jobs at once—the stool that becomes a table, for example, or the hollow bench you can stash your magazines in—so that you need less of it.

★ Keep your hoarding instinct in check; clutter is a small space's worst enemy.

# cooking & eating space

The kitchen can come in all shapes and sizes, but in a small living space it is more often than not the smallest room there is. It may be tucked into an awkward corner at the back of a house, stuffed into a side extension, or squeezed into an apartment corridor—wherever it is, it is bound to lack one thing: space. Having a small area to work with will limit you, of course (it's unlikely that you will be able to create that do-it-all living and cooking space, for example, unless you have the budget to knock down a few internal walls), but remember that a compact kitchen can be just as efficient and effective as a larger one, if not more so, if it is carefully planned and well designed. With simple units and slimline appliances, clever space-saving gadgets and pull-out or foldaway surfaces, you should be able to turn even a tiny or cramped kitchen space into a perfect mini machine for cooking in.

Garden designer Stephen Woodhams opened the back of his tiny row house and used what had been the side return for a new kitchen. Left open to the dining area and with glass walls and a glass roof, this little utility space is filled with light and seems far bigger than it really is. Storage space and appliances are all contained in an L-shaped row of dark wood units, giving a neat, sleek uniformity to the whole room.

## GENERAL PRINCIPLES

If you are building a kitchen from scratch, think carefully about the shape of the room and consider what kind of design would make the most of it. Units now come in so many different sizes and shapes that it shouldn't be difficult to find what you want. Before you start planning the room, however, it is worth bearing in mind these general space-saving principles:

**A built-in kitchen** rather than a collection of freestanding pieces is usually the best option in a small space.

**Avoiding units at eye level**, thus keeping the perimeter of the room in view, will make a kitchen seem less cramped.

**Extending the flooring**, the wall coloring, or even the countertop of the kitchen into an adjacent space will blur its boundaries and thus make it feel larger. (This, of course, will only work if the kitchen is open, or partially open, to another room.)

Choosing wider-than-average cabinets will broaden the room visually (and accommodate large-scale kitchen kit into the bargain).

Using glass for a kitchen wall or ceiling is a very effective way of opening the space up (though make sure to check with a structural surveyor that this can be done before you start), particularly if the room faces a garden or a terrace.

### KITCHEN LAYOUTS

There are several different ways to lay out a kitchen, so choose a format that will maximize the space you have at the same time as giving you all the utilities you need. Before you finally decide, think carefully about how you use your kitchen and pick a model that will suit the way you work.

The all-in-a-line look  This is perfect for a small but long kitchen or a cooking area that is incorporated into another room, because it takes up just one wall (make sure you have enough room to move around comfortably in front of it). The sink and the stove can be placed at either end of the counter (but not right in the corners; otherwise, you will risk banging your elbows on the wall), giving you preparation space in between; the dishwasher, refrigerator, and oven can be built in underneath. The one drawback of this kind of kitchen is that it does not

ABOVE  The owner of this small studio made the most of the dead space above a communal stairwell by buying it and building in it. Installing a chic contemporary kitchen on this new "floating" platform, she then had more space to play with in the living area. The kitchen, which is open on two sides, is compact but functional with simple units and built-in appliances.

RIGHT  Like a bridge across the top of the stairs, the kitchen is filled with light from the enormous window at the front of the property.

offer much storage space, so you will need to think of alternative storage areas if you have a lot of equipment (see Storage, overleaf).

**The galley** A row of units on each side of a room with a corridor in between, the galley is a neat solution in a small kitchen. It offers a fair amount of counter and storage space, and is easy to use. If you have a very narrow kitchen, however, it may not be practical; the "corridor" needs to be big enough to allow access to under-the-counter units.

**The L-shape** This is a good solution for a long, thin kitchen where there may not be enough room for units on both sides. Place the stove on the short part of the L, the sink, utilities, and counter on the long, and you have a format that is ergonomic and easy to work with.

RIGHT **Even the smallest space can accommodate a kitchen. The owners of this property have chosen to incorporate a tiny utility area into their dining area rather than giving the kitchen a room of its own. Cleverly enclosed inside a floor-to-ceiling cupboard on one side of the space, the cooking area can be concealed when not in use, but opens up easily to become part of the dining area. Though small, the "room" has all the kitchen requisites: a stove, a sink, wall-mounted storage space, and even a microwave.**

**The U-shape and beyond** A kitchen with units wrapping around three or even four walls is not usually the best solution in a small space because it gives you little freedom to move in the center of the room. If this is your only option, however, it is best to ignore the "no units at eye level" advice and place the appliances you use frequently (the oven, the fridge) in this higher position where access will be easier. If you can, put the dining table and chairs elsewhere so the kitchen can become just a compact machine for cooking in (see pages 24–31).

**The island** Although not always a possibility in a tiny, self-contained kitchen, the island can work brilliantly if the kitchen is open to an adjacent room (indeed, it can act as the room divider here—see pages 52–59). A well designed island unit can accommodate everything from

If you just hold onto the essentials, you should be able to find a home for everything, even in a tiny kitchen.

cupboards and stove to the kitchen trash can and, with four separate sides, several people can use the thing at once without getting in each other's way. For ultimate flexibility, put the island unit on wheels so you can move it out of the way when it is not in use (not a viable option, of course, if the island incorporates your stove). If it is fixed, place the island on a pedestal to give a "floating," space-enhancing effect.

## STORAGE

This is a particularly key issue in the kitchen, where you have much to store and little space in which to do it. A good starting point is to pare down your collection of gadgets by giving away anything you no longer need (that old sandwich toaster, for instance) or by stashing things you use only irregularly (a fondue set, perhaps) in longer-term storage space (an attic or a cellar, say). If you just hold onto the essentials, you should be able to find a home for everything, even in a tiny kitchen.

**Built-in storage** Get all the white goods—washing machine, dishwasher, microwave, and so on—built into the structure of your kitchen if possible. This way, you can create a seamless row of units with everything tucked neatly out of sight, and because nothing extraneous will intrude on the space, your kitchen will feel bigger. For a sleek and uniform finish (always good for that clutter-free look), try to make sure that each of your appliances matches the rest of the units (all stainless steel, for example); if they don't, consider hiding them behind matching panels.

**Secret storage** There are lots of neglected storage areas in the kitchen, and they come into their own when space is short. Consider, for example, concealing things in drawers behind the kick-plates at the bottom of your units (fit them with spring-loaded catches so they will open with a nudge of the foot); hide cookie sheets underneath the oven, cookbooks in the dead space above the fridge. Use the inside of a cupboard door for a spice rack or construct a series of thin shelves within a dividing wall (as long as it is not a supporting one). The key is to make the most of the space you have and not to waste even a bit of it.

**Stolen space** If your kitchen is so small that you have no storage space at all, borrow space from the adjacent rooms. Create kitchen drawers that back, secretly, into a bedroom closet, for example; extend a

Kitchens make huge demands on our storage space. We need shelves for tableware; cupboards for food; drawers for utensils; racks for pans. In a small space, finding a home for all these is a challenge, but it can be done. The key is to build in as much as you can and to make the most of every bit of space. Buy specially designed corner units for awkward bits of your kitchen so you can access them easily (LEFT) or invest in extendable racks which should more than double capacity (RIGHT). And use walls or ceilings for open storage: hang racks or hooks for pans above the stove, for example, or erect extra shelves (ABOVE).

LEFT AND ABOVE **In a small home, it is likely that all the appliances—even the washing machine—will end up in the kitchen. Although it may cost more at the outset, it is worth incorporating them into the structure of your kitchen (if there is room) to create a tight, uncluttered layout. Try to give the appliances the same finish as the rest of the units so that, visually, they won't stand out, for this should make the room feel sleeker and more spacious. In this minimal modern kitchen, the owners have tucked everything from the oven to the microwave behind uniform blond doors.**

cupboard under the stairs; accommodate a fridge in the dining room (see pages 46–51). Ingenious tricks like these will help you to create space and reduce clutter in the kitchen.

**Wall and ceiling storage** Using walls and ceilings for storage is a clever solution in any room with a small floor area. Try to buy equipment and appliances that can be mounted on the wall to free worktop and floor space (these days everything from radiators to ironing boards and kitchen scales can be wall-mounted), though don't go over the top or the room will look cluttered. And maximize the potential of high ceilings if you have them by putting up racks and rails on which you can hang pots, pans, and utensils, or suspend modular storage units from an overhead track. One London-based couple even created a winch system for their dining table so that it could be pulled up to the ceiling when not in use.

**Space-saving kitchen kit** Because so many of our kitchens are small and because, today, we need to fit so much into them (dishwasher, microwaves, rice cookers, et al.), there are now countless space-saving

designs on the market. There are a host of slimline and mini appliances, for example, which can be squeezed into small spaces—you can even buy a portable one-ring gas burner. There are fold-down and pull-out countertops; extendable corner units and expanding storage racks—all of which can be shut out of sight when not in use. There are also double-up designs, which allow two jobs to be done in one place, such as the sink that can be topped with a chopping board or the storage unit that can be turned into a kitchen table. Just a few of these ingenious gadgets will give you the flexibility to liberate your space without sacrificing all those mod cons. They won't cost the earth and may make all the difference.

**Makeover tricks** If you can't refit or change the design of your tiny kitchen, don't despair. There are simple things that you can do to make it feel bigger. Use mirrored tiles behind the sink, for example; paint cabinet doors in a reflective glossy paint (or replace them with stainless steel); illuminate areas below and above the units to give the impression of continuing space. See Color, Texture, & Lighting, page 120, for more.

# SPACE SAVERS FOR **KITCHENS & DINING ROOMS**

★ Rationalize your kitchen gear and get rid of anything you don't use frequently.

★ Invest in mini and slimline appliances.

★ Create pull-out and foldaway surfaces that can be concealed when not in use.

★ Use the walls for storage.

★ Hang racks and rails from the ceiling for storing pots, pans, and utensils.

★ Put shelves inside as many units as you can (even the one under the sink) to give yourself twice the storage area.

★ Use the backs of doors for spice racks or utensil storage.

★ Put drawers at the bottom of your units (behind the kick-plates) for storing dish towels, oven gloves, or baking sheets.

★ Buy a chopping board that fits over the top of the sink, making the most of dead space and hiding the mess.

★ Make kitchen surfaces shiny and reflective to increase the sensation of space.

# working space

More and more of us are working from home these days, but few of our homes have the space to accommodate an office. In a large house, the working area is often squeezed into the smallest room or the corner of a larger one. In a small house, of course, the situation is even worse, with offices shoved into tiny, cramped spaces—not places that make for a healthy and effective working environment. What can be done? The key is to create a sense of space and a comfortable atmosphere wherever your home office is sited, and to make the most of flexible office furniture and equipment. If it's well thought out, even the tiniest space can become a functional, efficient, and pleasant place to work.

## THE TINY ONE-ROOM OFFICE
If you work in a very small room, think of ways to make it seem bigger. Do all you can to maximize daylight (install a skylight if you need to) and create a highly organized office system so you can eliminate clutter.

**The desk** Choose a desk that fits neatly against a wall or in a corner, or—even better—get a worktop made to fit your space exactly. Don't waste the area underneath: use it for a filing cabinet (if it fits), boxes of books, or computer equipment. Alternatively, invest in a multilevel desk which, like a terraced garden, has a number of staggered surfaces to give you a good amount of desktop storage without taking up much room.

**Storage** This is particularly crucial in a mini office, and whatever storage system you choose, it should be very organized so you know where everything is and can put away your work easily. Built-in cupboards provide the neatest solution because you can shut your clutter away. If you have shelves, invest in uniform box files and storage boxes (label them clearly), so that when they are lined up, they will look neat.

**Computer equipment** In a small space it can be hard to accommodate all the technological kit, but do your best to keep it under control. Hide the printer under the desk or in a cupboard (internal sockets would be very useful here), and stack up the rest as efficiently as you can. If you have little room to move, place your monitor on a pivoting arm so you can easily change its position.

**Bits and pieces** Paper, pens, diaries, notebooks—the office is always full of clutter. Keep it at bay by only having out what you need and storing the rest out of sight or in a row of baskets or boxes at the back of your worktop. One neat solution for coping with letters and messages (particularly if you haven't space for an in-tray) is to create a giant pinboard in front of your desk (it could fill a whole wall if necessary). Keep it orderly and organized, and you should never lose anything again.

OPPOSITE **Squeezed into an unsuitable corner or forced to share part of another room, the home office is often the room that suffers most in a tiny home. However small your workstation, however, make it efficient with a good desk, an ergonomic chair, a suitable light, and lots of storage.**

ABOVE AND LEFT **Exploit vertical space to the full by stacking up storage spots at the front of your desk. And wherever you place your office, try to make sure your work is screened from view. Here a bead curtain hides the desk from the main living area.**

## UNUSUAL LOCATIONS

If you haven't got a spare room for your home office, consider where else you could create an effective working area. If you have high ceilings and a reasonable budget, think about constructing a mezzanine in a living room or bedroom. It needn't be big to accommodate a workstation, and it would give you a self-contained office space. Alternatively, if you've room, you could build an extra level at the top of the stairs or in the hall. If you have very little spare space, create a series of floor-to-ceiling cupboards against a wall and enclose your entire office—bar the chair, obviously—within it (see page 40). This way you can open it up when you are working and shut it away when you are not. Similarly, the "office in a box"—

OPPOSITE AND BELOW  With a worktop and row of cabinets on one side, this flexible space makes an efficient home office, but pull out the convertible sofa and shut away the files, and it becomes a clean-lined, comfortable bedroom. To maximize this dual-purpose potential, the room has been furnished neutrally and has features, such as the open box shelves, that work well in both roles.

RIGHT AND FAR RIGHT  Frosted glass doors separate this room from the rest of the apartment, while a tiny bathroom provides bathing facilities.

Make sure you can hide your work away once you have finished for the day (if you have open shelves, screen them off at bedtime behind a curtain).

something a few ingenious suppliers are offering—allows you to access your working space as and when (and where) you need it.

## SHARED SPACES

Many of us are forced to work in another room—at the end of the dining-room table, for example, or on one side of the bedroom. Doubling up a room's functions like this will be a problem if you allow one role to intrude on the other (leaving office papers all over the bedroom floor, for example), but if the arrangement of the room is planned carefully, it can work well. The office in the bedroom can be a good combination since the room's functions won't conflict (it can be one by day, the other by night), but make sure you can hide your work away once you have finished for the day (if you have open shelves, screen them off at bedtime behind a partition or curtain). Good storage is essential (the floor-to-ceiling cupboards mentioned above would be perfect), and to make things easier for yourself, try to incorporate flexible features into the structure of the room: a pull-down bed, perhaps, or a flap-down desk that can disappear when you need it to. If you haven't the budget for foldaway fixtures, make sure you choose furniture adaptable enough to fit both roles: a plain desk that can double as a dressing table, for example, or a bedside table-filing cabinet.

# SPACE SAVERS
## FOR **WORK ROOMS**

★ Get your office in order: nothing looks more cluttered than random piles of paper.

★ Create a working wall by running filing cabinets and a work surface with an integral desk along the length of a room (see pages 14–15). Even better, enclose it in a series of cupboards if you can.

★ Buy uniform box files for storing your work.

★ Fit sockets inside cupboards so you can stack up your computer gear behind closed doors.

★ Don't waste space: it is amazing what you can fit under a desk.

★ Create a giant pinboard for messages and memos.

★ If your workstation is in another room, shut it away or screen it off when it is not in use.

★ Create thin drawers beneath your desk for hiding desktop clutter.

★ Invest in new space-saving office designs—a multilevel desk or an office in a box, for example.

★ Don't buy dull office furniture: choose pieces that would look good anywhere.

# bathing space

In many small homes, bathrooms have a rough time of it. Stuffed into small, airless rooms or squeezed into awkward corners, they are not, generally speaking, the sybaritic spaces we would like them to be. Treated in the past more like a utility room than a pleasure dome, today's bathroom tends to be filled with an ill-planned medley of functional fixtures and cluttered with an increasing load of bathing "essentials"— a particular problem to cope with in a confined space.

There are things that we can do to improve the situation, however. If you are building a bathroom from scratch or completely restructuring an old one, you can work even the tiniest space to your advantage. If you haven't a gap for a shower cubicle, create a wet room, which needs no such division. If you've no space for an standard bathtub, buy a small one or get one built in to fit the available area exactly (see pages 18–23). Consider, too, opening the bathroom (partially, at least) to an adjacent bedroom so it feels larger; or screening the space with frosted glass panels rather than a solid wall to increase the light.

If you have neither the budget nor the time to change your bathroom structurally, make the best of what you have. Think of new places to store all that clutter, bring in mirrors to increase the sense of space, and use a few decorative tricks to make the room seem larger than it really is. Last, and most important, be strict with your toiletries: buy only what you need and get rid of bottles, cans, and tubes as soon as they are empty. If it is properly planned, cleverly finished, and well managed, even the tiniest bathroom can become a sanctuary.

RIGHT **This bathing wall in a very narrow bathroom space incorporates all the necessities—shower, toilet, basin, and tub— in a linear arrangement. Glass panels surround the shower, making a cubicle to provide protection from splashes without foreshortening the room visually. The top half of the wall is covered in mirror-fronted panels, to reflect available light.**

LEFT **Creating a mini bathroom can be a good way of saving upstairs space in a one-bedroom home. Here a tiny bathroom has been created without compromising sleeping space. The door is frosted glass, to give privacy without shutting out the light, and the large mirror on the back wall makes the room feel almost double its size. Borrowing space from the bedroom and kept uncluttered, it feels neither cramped nor confined.**

## SPACE-SAVING BATHROOM KIT

**The hard stuff** If you have little space, it is a good idea to invest in smaller-than-average baths and basins. Tubs come in all shapes and sizes, so choose one that fits your needs or get one made to measure for an awkward space. Square or even triangular tubs work well in a tight corner, but remember that they need to be deeper than average rectangular ones to give you adequate water. If you can, sink such a tub into the floor so it doesn't take up too much vertical space.

A shower, of course, is perfect for a tiny bathroom (indeed, it might be all you can fit in). Pick a streamlined design and avoid bulky cubicles and curtains (a half wall fixed to the side of a bathtub makes a good screen). Choose a toilet, too, that is simply shaped and not too cumbersome. Corner and wall-mounted designs work well in a small space.

If you are feeling adventurous, seek out more esoteric space-saving bathing devices, many of which come from Japan. Quirky designs on offer include everything from toilets topped with an integrated basin (the refill water can thus be used for washing your hands) to retractable shower stalls (a circular plastic curtain descends from the ceiling to surround a central shower rod). The Japanese have even produced a "unit bath" in which bathtub, basin, and toilet fixtures have been ready molded in prefabricated plastic and fiberglass.

**Fixtures** Choose the simplest designs you can and get them built in wherever possible. The shower head, for example, can be sunk into the ceiling; the bath spout and faucets incorporated into the wall, freeing up space and giving a generally less cluttered look. If the floor area is particularly tight, radiators and towel rods can be wall mounted, making the most of the dead space above the toilet, for example, or beside the bathtub (see pages 32–37).

### STORAGE

This is always an issue in the bathroom, and if you don't address it effectively, you can end up with surfaces littered with plastic bottles and toothpaste tubes—not what you want in a tiny space. The key is to incorporate as much storage space as posssible into the room so all the clutter can be kept out of sight. If you think laterally and use every bit of the available space, this is simpler than it sounds.

**In-built** Built-in storage solutions have an advantage over their freestanding relatives because they don't stand out or intrude into the space so much, particularly if you place them carefully. If you construct a row of wall-to-wall cabinets above the doorway, for example, it will remain hidden as you enter the room but offer plenty of space for towels and washcloths (give it sliding rather than swing doors for a sleek and space-saving finish). Consider building a cupboard under the basin

RIGHT AND BELOW **Showers and bathtubs can be built into awkward spaces as long as you can make the plumbing work. Here a rounded unit has been created to accommodate a shower, basin, and bathtub. Half colorful mosaic and half glass block tiles, which screen the room from view but let light through, this mini bathroom fits a lot into a tiny space. There is even a soap dish attached to the glass wall in the shower.**

Open the bathroom to an adjacent bedroom, or screen the space with frosted glass panels rather than a solid wall to increase the light.

or in the gap at the end of a bathtub—indeed, use any available awkward space for storage.

If you haven't the room for cupboards or want something less obvious, your fixtures can include integral storage solutions. A built-in bathtub could have a shelf around its perimeter; a mirror, placed flush against the wall, could conceal storage space behind (if your walls are thick enough); a basin unit could hide a niche for bathroom bits and pieces (see pages 43–44). And look out for smaller space-saving designs: tiles with in-built soap dishes or toothbrush racks, for example, or a shower head with hooks for hanging bath products and shampoo. Double-up devices can make all the difference in a tiny space.

**Ingenious** When you are trying to maximize space in a small area, it is worth considering more unconventional storage ideas. If you

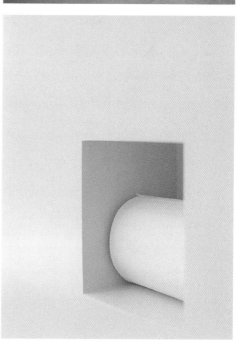

have no space for a cabinet, why not erect a series of glass shelves against the window? This will give you room for bathroom stuff and won't block out the light. Or how about installing a fold-down counter over the toilet tank (if it is low enough), or even over the bathtub if it is not used frequently? Perhaps it could double as a sometime bathroom seat.

## DECORATIVE TRICKS

If you don't have the budget to change your bathroom structurally, or if you live in a rented space and can't make structural alterations, think of simple decorative tricks to make the room look larger. Put a giant mirror on the ceiling, for example, to double the space visually (see page 31), or—on a smaller scale—cover your splashback with mirrored tiles. And keep the surfaces shiny; the more light you can bring into a bathroom, the better.

ABOVE **Wet rooms make sense in a small property because they require fewer fixtures than a conventional bathroom (no need for shower cubicles, for example). Waterproofing the room at the outset, however, can be costly, so get several quotes and check your budget before you start.**

RIGHT, TOP AND CENTER **This glass screen between bed and bathroom can change from clear (space-enhancing) to opaque (private) at the flick of a switch.**

RIGHT **A brilliantly neat solution for the toilet paper, which does away with the need for fussy roll holders.**

# SPACE SAVERS
## FOR **BATHROOMS**

★ Put a mirror on the bathroom ceiling to double the space.

★ Build in bathroom fixtures where possible.

★ Hide all your toiletries and bathroom clutter behind closed doors.

★ Use awkward spaces for storage.

★ Erect a corner seat that can double as a shelf when not in use.

★ Invest in smaller-than-standard bathroom fixtures or get some custommade to fit your space exactly.

★ Wall-mount as much as you can—radiators, cabinets, even the toilet.

★ If you haven't the space for a big mirror, cover your splashback in mirrored tiles or buy a mirrored wall cabinet that does two jobs at once.

★ Use reflective surfaces where you can: shiny things bring in more light.

★ Avoid cumbersome shower cabinets and messy curtains: a sleek frosted glass panel will give a much cleaner result.

Furniture that disappears when you don't need it is ideal for any small space, and the wall bed has to be one of the best. It works particularly well in any room that has to do two jobs at once and brings maximum convertibility and value to any small home. In this diminutive basement apartment, the architect's design created a pull-down bed that shuts away into a cupboard when not in use. With the façade a series of colorful panels (some of which provide easy-access storage), the bed is cleverly concealed.

# sleeping space

The most personal and private part of any interior, the bedroom is a space we particularly want to get right. The bathroom may be cramped and the kitchen cluttered, but here we want a haven, somewhere neat, tranquil, and relaxing. We spend more or less half our lives in the place, after all. The good news is that turning the bedroom into a sanctuary is more easily achieved in a small home than in a large one. There is something inherently cozy about a tiny sleeping space, so if that is what you have, maximize its nestlike qualities.

Before you start, however, there are practical considerations to take into account. Where can you stash your collection of clothes? How can you fit two beds into a space built for one? Where can you store your bed linen? Take time to resolve these issues (and you can), and you'll be well on your way to creating the ultimate mini comfort zone.

### BEDS
Think first about how you use the bedroom. If you are very short of space, chances are that you will need it for more than one function—for nighttime sleeping and daytime working, perhaps. If this is the case, you'll want a bed that doubles as a sofa, say, or that disappears when

not in use. Equally, you may want to accommodate a spare bed for overnight guests that can be hidden away when not required. These days, there is a wealth of bedroom furniture on the market, with products to suit every location and requirement, so see what is out there and choose whatever is right for you.

**Bunk beds**  Good for kids, but remember that you need a fairly high ceiling for the person sleeping on top to be comfortable. If you are kitting out a room for just one child, consider a platform bed (just the top bunk) that incorporates a working or playing area underneath.

**Convertible sofas**  The original flexible piece of furniture, these are still a good solution if you need extra floor space during the day or as instant guest beds. Futons are a good alternative.

**Wall beds**  The bed that can be pulled down from the wall when needed is a brilliant solution in a tiny room, freeing floor space at other times. Several specialized companies offer advisory services and produce a variety of designs. If you opt for one of these, however, you will need somewhere to store your linen and pillow when the bed is shut away.

You could use the area beneath the bed deck as an office or private sitting area; if not, consider using some of it for a closet (walk-in, if there's space).

**Fold-up, trundle, and stacking beds** These work well as instant guest or occasional-use beds, and can be hidden underneath a conventional bed when not in use. One of the best new designs is the award-winning Snoozy bed by Inflate—a five-piece modular system with molded legs that pull apart for easy storage.

**Retracting beds** A more idiosyncratic option that you will probably need to get custom-built, these beds are winched up to the ceiling when not in use. Either crank- or electrically operated, they can only be hung on a ceiling that can withstand their weight.

## MEZZANINES

If you have a studio with no separate bedroom or if you need to create an extra sleeping area, for example, for guests or children, consider erecting a mezzanine. These gallerylike spaces make great bed decks, but will only work if you have high enough ceilings to accommodate the extra level comfortably (there should be a minimum of 5 feet (1.5 meters) above the platform for it to function effectively). Get advice from a structural engineer before you embark on building, and think

**ABOVE LEFT Another impromptu sleeping solution—a folding bed that can be stashed away in a sleek wooden storage box-bench when not in use. Hollows at each end provide extra space for storage.**

**ABOVE AND OPPOSITE If you have more vertical space than lateral, exploit those high ceilings by placing your bedroom on a mezzanine. In this small sleeping space, a series of storage cupboards have been fronted with mirrored panels to double the space visually, while a wooden platform acts as bookshelf, bedside, and dressing table.**

carefully about the best place to position it. Remember that a mezzanine is an open space, so take the noise factor into account. A bed deck might look good above your living area, for example, but it will be hard to sleep if people are chatting below.

A mezzanine bedroom will not be large, particularly if the room it is in is small, but this need not be a disadvantage. If you are very short of space, why not make the mezzanine all bed (see pages 10–17)—a sensible option as long as you have room for bedroom storage elsewhere. Buy a bed to fit if you can or construct your own, using the floor area as a bed base and simply topping it with a mattress (it is a good idea to choose a mattress slightly smaller than the base or floor, so the surround can act as a surface for bedside clutter—books, glasses, alarm clocks).

In addition to creating an extra "room," the mezzanine can also help to divide the space below (particularly useful in an open-plan studio such as Guy Hills's). If it is large enough, you could use the area beneath the bed deck as an office or a more private sitting area; if not, consider using some of it for a closet (walk-in, if there's space). If you have a very confined area, use a ladder to access the mezzanine level. If you have room, put in stairs and don't forget to exploit them for storage. Box steps can provide a good amount of cupboard space (indeed, they can even accommodate a closet) and needn't take up too much room.

## STORAGE

This is something we are nearly always short of in the bedroom. In a tiny bedroom, storage needs to be very well planned if you are to avoid clothes and clutter taking over. Consider your individual requirements (do you have to find a home for a hundred pairs of shoes, for example, or have you a giant make-up collection that won't fit anywhere else?) and then select storage solutions that will work for you. The key rule is, you always need more storage than you think.

**Closet space** The best advice is to get them built in. Much as you might hanker after a glamorous old French armoire, these freestanding closets tend to be cumbersome rather than capacious, and in a tiny bedroom they simply take up too much space. The neatest idea is to construct a seamless wall of floor-to-ceiling cupboards across the width of your room. Try painting the doors the same color as the walls to make the unit still more invisible or, even better, give them a mirrored surface to double the space visually. You can then customize the inside to accommodate everything from dresses and suits to shoes and bed linen. Put shelves right at the top for stowing things you use irregularly (skiwear or hats, say); create vertical storage—at each end, perhaps—for sweaters and shoes; install a double hanging rod in one section to give you twice the suit-stashing capacity. If you haven't the time to create such a tailormade storage system for yourself, there are companies that will do it for you. Such personal service, of course, doesn't come cheap.

If your bedroom is too small for a wall of storage, make the best of what you have. Make an ad hoc closet by putting a hanging rod and floor-level boxes in an unused alcove, and conceal your clothes with a screen or a curtain. Create hanging space behind the bed (if you have a large headboard), or exploit the vertical potential of a ladder for storing sweaters or even shoes.

**Underbed drawers** Using the dead space under the bed, these are great for bedroom

Whether you choose a freestanding armoire (ABOVE LEFT) or a more ad hoc solution, such as this curtained alcove (ABOVE RIGHT), make sure you give yourself enough storage space so that all clothes and clutter can be hidden from view.

Make an ad hoc closet with a hanging rod and floor-level boxes, and conceal your clothes with a screen or curtain.

storage. Buy drawers on castors for easy access or raise the level of the bed to fit a whole series of drawers underneath (see pages 36–37). A new take on the platform bed, this will give you copious amounts of storage without intruding on the room's floor space.

**Display areas** In a tiny bedroom, it is unlikely that you will have room for a dressing table or even a chest, so think of other places for your photographs, jewelry box, antique hand mirror, or whatever you want to have on show. Free the floor space by making the most of your walls. Put a narrow shelf above a radiator, for example, or erect a series of box shelves (like overblown pigeonholes), which can hold things both on top and inside.

ABOVE If your bedroom is reasonably long but has little space for a chest or closet, erecting a wall of cupboards at one end of the room can be the best solution. Stretching from floor to ceiling, it will give you a good amount of storage, but won't be as obtrusive as a freestanding piece of furniture, particularly if you paint the cupboard doors the same color as the surrounding walls. Inside, create the storage system you need, mixing hanging rods (two deep for twice the capacity) with shelves or drawers for sweaters and shoes.

# SPACE SAVERS
## FOR **BEDROOMS**

★ For a dual-purpose room, invest in a wall bed that can be shut away when you don't need it.

★ If you have the room and the budget, erect a mezzanine to use as an extra bedroom.

★ Pare down your collection of clothes and accessories. In a small room, there is no space for things you no longer use or wear.

★ Use a narrow shelf or even a mantelpiece as a dressing table and top with a mirror to complete the picture.

★ If you can, create a wall of floor-to-ceiling cupboards. They provide lots of surreptitious storage space.

★ Take time to customize your closet. If everything has a place, it will be far easier to keep clutter at bay.

★ Cover your closet doors with mirrors so your room will look twice the size.

★ If you haven't room for a bedside table, buy a bed with an integral shelf for bedtime clutter (books, clocks, radios, and so on).

★ Erect a low shelf along one wall of the room (or on each side of the bed). In addition to functioning as a bedside table and occasional seat, this also could house books and magazines underneath. And it won't clutter the room at eye level.

★ Buy drawers that can be hidden under the bed for storing bed linen and clothes.

By extending his tiny house with a conservatory at the back, Stephen Woodhams established a strong link between outdoor and indoor space. Divided from the main house by giant floor-to-ceiling windows and decorated with similar materials and colors, the garden feels just like an extension of the dining and living areas inside, and the interior feels bigger than it is.

# **outdoor** connections

One of the best ways of making an interior feel more spacious is to maximize its connections with the outdoors. A view of the outside world, framed by a window or a door, draws the eye beyond the boundaries of a home and makes it, quite simply, feel bigger. The architect behind Ben and Geraldine Atfield's mini skyscraper (see pages 18–23) took this idea to an extreme by using glass for the entire façade of the house, but creating a connection on a smaller scale can work just as well. You could install floor-to-ceiling windows in a room that overlooks a garden, perhaps, or create an internal courtyard in the heart of your home. You could simply enlarge or add an extra window or two or put in a skylight. One last thing: you don't need to have a big garden to capitalize on those outdoor outlooks; views of a roof terrace, a tiny plot, an urban landscape, or even someone else's garden will all help to make your interior seem larger.

## WINDOWS AND WALLS

Just a glimpse of garden or sky will extend your perception of space and make even a tiny room feel less claustrophobic, so think about upping your quota of windows to bring the outside in. Try to create a view right through your interior if you can (see pages 52–59), which will maximize the feeling of spaciousness and exploit whatever external space you have. If you have a roof terrace, make sure it can be seen from inside as much as possible. Substitute glass sliding doors for walls if you can (see pages 24–31) or create a long slice of window right across the relevant wall. If you've a tiny row house leading onto a tiny urban yard, open up the back as much as you can by creating a wall of glass or by erecting a conservatory and using it as part of your internal space. If you have built into a side return to give yourself more downstairs room (a common trick in Victorian houses), make the extension—walls and ceiling—all glass. It will give you a lot more light and make the entire ground floor seem far less confined.

If your surroundings are not particularly picturesque, use skylights rather than extra windows to give that connection with outdoors. And place them where you can see them—in a bathroom ceiling, for example, to give you views of the sky as you bathe. And consider using

Just a glimpse of garden or sky will extend your perception of space and make a room feel less claustrophobic.

**OPPOSITE AND LEFT A view of the outdoors can make even the smallest urban living space feel expansive, by drawing the eye away from the confines of the interior. Here, large sash windows frame sections of a flower-covered balcony, bringing in both light and a feeling of space.**

**ABOVE RIGHT It doesn't matter whether you are surrounded by country fields or a gritty urban landscape, any view of the outside world will extend the sense of space inside your home. Glimpsed through picture windows, this cityscape seems very much part of the interior.**

portholes if you have little space; they will not only give you graphic views of the outdoors, they will become an interior design feature, too.

### EXTENDING THE INTERIOR

Once you have established a connection with outdoors, it is a good idea to create a decorative link between the internal and the external space, to blur the distinction between each (this is only possible if you have your own personal outdoor area—a roof terrace or a backyard, of course). Creating such indoor-outdoor space is a clever way of making both house and yard feel bigger than they really are, and there are several ways of doing it. You could pick out colors from the interior to use for the outdoor furniture, perhaps, or match the tone of your living room wall with a flower color. You could use similar wall finishes or even the same flooring for the house and the garden terrace.

### USING GLASS INSIDE

Extend the use of glass to the interior, too. Frosted or colored glass panels will divide up internal space effectively, but seem less solid than conventional walls (and thus less intrusive) and not block the light.

# MAXIMIZING OUTDOOR CONNECTIONS

★ Install floor-to-ceiling French doors in a room that overlooks a yard or terrace, so it becomes part of the internal space.

★ Remove internal doors if you can, so the outdoors can be glimpsed even from the front of your home.

★ Substitute see-through barriers for solid ones where you can. A glass roof or wall will instantly bring the outside in.

★ If you haven't much space, install narrow windows or even a porthole to frame a section of the surrounding landscape.

★ Maximize the sunlight: enlarge the windows and use frosted or clear glass for partitions inside.

★ Create a decorative link between indoor and outdoor space by using the same colors or materials for both.

★ Bring nature inside: flowers, twigs, or even a pile of pebbles will give you that outdoor connection.

★ If your outlook isn't pretty, install a skylight instead of a window. This will bring in the light and give you unsullied outdoor views.

solutions

# dividing space

In a small house or apartment, it is tempting to keep the interior as open as possible to maximize what little space there is, but this is not always the best solution. By leaving a studio apartment, for example, completely open-plan, you draw attention to the fact that it is just one undifferentiated space, and it will be stuck with just one identity. If you divide it into different zones, it will instantly become more interesting and, paradoxically, seem larger. Without the perimeter of the studio in view and with suggestions of space beyond a dividing wall or partition, say, the eye can be conned into thinking that a place is bigger than it is.

You don't want to divide a tiny home into a series of boxy rooms, of course, so think of ways that you can delineate space without confining it. Instead of solid floor-to-ceiling walls, consider more partial partitions—a half wall, a sliding door, or a screen, for example—or divide up your interior decoratively by using different flooring, lighting, or color in different places. This can be particularly effective in a multipurpose room (a living-dining room, perhaps), where you may want to isolate the different parts of the room to give each definition.

If your home is already divided with walls that you can't or don't want to remove, make them seem less solid by creating an archway (square-topped unless you want that 1970s Greek restaurant look) or by knocking out holes at strategic intervals (get advice from a structural engineer to make sure the wall can take it). Internal windows can help bring light into a dark area and also, by creating a view through into an adjacent space, will help to make a room feel bigger.

## STRUCTURAL DIVIDERS

**Walls**  Solid floor-to-ceiling walls are not what you want in a small area, but waist-high or half walls can help you divide space without losing the sense of it. Place such a partition between a kitchen and dining room, for example, and you will contain the cooking area while retaining a sweep of open space at eye level. Enclose the head of the bathtub with a plane of frosted glass or mosaic (make it tall enough for modesty, but not up to the ceiling) and you can create an effective shower screen without the need for a space-consuming cubicle.

Materials for any such permanent partition matter, so consider your options carefully. While you may want a solid plane in the kitchen (to hide the mess), elsewhere glass or even

OPPOSITE  **In a small home, you want to divide space without confining it, so rather than solid walls, think of more flexible and fluid solutions. Curtains, for example, can be used very effectively to separate different parts of your interior as and when you need to, and they can also help to soften a stark or minimal space.**

RIGHT  **Use glass for fixed partitions to let the light through (BELOW), or opt for something more flexible, such as a sliding door or wall (ABOVE).**

BELOW  **In this dining-cooking area, the kitchen is tucked behind a neat waist-high wall, which means that the cook can chat with guests while he or she works, but kitchen mess is hidden from view.**

Designer Lloyd Schwan took out several of the internal walls of this small New York apartment, turning it into a more or less open-plan space. The biggest area (RIGHT) is now split between a lounging zone and a dining zone (isolated on an island of carpet), while the kitchen is tucked to one side (LEFT). Wanting to create some separation between the eating and cooking areas, Schwan retained the dividing wall here, but carved out an internal window and a door to keep the two partially connected. With rounded corners framing pastel-colored units, it gives a funky retro look to the place.

colored Plexiglas can work well and will allow light through (always useful in a small space).

For a more flexible, hi-tech solution, consider installing a sliding acoustic wall as the Mody-Clarks did (see pages 38–45), which can be hidden in an adjacent wall when it is not in use. This will give you the luxury of closing off part of your interior when you want.

**Doors** If hinged doors are the enemy of the small space (they simply take up too much of it), then sliding, folding, and swing doors are its best friends. Not only do they take up far less room than a conventional door, if they are well designed, they should also fit neatly into the surrounding architecture when they are not in use, giving a sleek and streamlined finish.

**The swing or pivoting door** These work best when they do two jobs at once (i.e., by enclosing two different areas, depending on which way they are swung). See the Mody-Clarks's house (pages 38–45) for inspiration.

**The folding or accordion door** Like giant shutters, pull-out and expandable doors are perfect for dividing a large dual-purpose room as long as there is enough space to conceal the device when it is not in use. Choose a design that is easy to manipulate and not too heavy, so you won't neglect using it.

**The sliding door** The perfect substitute for the average door, this works wherever there is space to accommodate it (remember when

THIS PAGE By removing the ceilings above the living area in this Italian apartment, a previously dark and dingy space has been filled with light.

OPPOSITE In this tiny London apartment, space has been created for an office by placing the bedroom on a new mezzanine platform, accessed by a flight of steep and sculptural wooden stairs. Dividing space vertically like this is a brilliant solution anywhere the ceilings are high.

not in use, it will need an area of the same size or greater to rest against). Small sliding doors can usually be hung just from a track at the top; larger doors may need a floor guide, too.

**Mezzanines** If you have high ceilings and want to create more space, consider erecting a mezzanine. By dividing just a section of a room horizontally, a mezzanine need not intrude too much on your existing space and will give you an extra room without the need for a costly extension (see the Sleeping Space chapter, pages 76–83, for more details).

**Using the floor** One of the best ways of dividing space in a small home is to raise the level of the floor—but only in certain places. Although it might seem counterproductive to reduce the volume of a tiny room in any way,

> By dividing just a section of a room horizontally, a mezzanine need not intrude too much on your existing space and will give you an extra room.

this can be a very effective method of visually separating two different areas—a dining area and a sitting area, for example—and the change in level doesn't have to be great. Even 4in (10cm) or so would do the trick, though you can make it greater if you want the added benefit of underfloor storage space. It is a good idea to use different flooring for the upper and the lower areas to provide definition and also to draw attention to the level change for practical reasons. You don't want to make the two zones too different, however (it is one room, after all), so think of ways to integrate the raised area into the main space, by using the same wall coloring, perhaps, or putting similar objects on display.

Using a fluid and flexible partition—such as this bead curtain that separates office space from the main living area—is an effective way of dividing up space in a small house. Not only does it take up little room, it can easily be removed or tied back when it is no longer needed.

### FLEXIBLE PARTITIONS

**Curtains and blinds** Inexpensive and relatively easy to fit, fabric drapes or blinds make good space dividers. Hung from the ceiling, they can create an instant partition between a sitting and a dining area, for example, or can be pulled down to conceal a work space when it's not in use. Blinds are the neatest solution because they generally disappear into their own fixture, but curtains can work well if they can be neatly stored (a hidden track works well) and will give a softer, more fluid result. Curtains or blinds can also be used effectively to hide the clutter of an open shelving system and thus give a more streamlined look to a room.

**Using the furniture** Choosing furniture that can do two jobs at once is always worthwhile in a small space, and many larger pieces can make good impromptu room dividers. A bookcase, for example, works particularly well (especially if you can access the shelves from both sides), because it splits up space and provides additional storage; but many other pieces—a sofa, a kitchen island, a row of stools—can also create a visual partition between different areas of a room. If you are completely overhauling your interior, consider constructing a purpose-built piece of furniture that will divide space as well— a closet "wall" between two bedrooms, perhaps, or a double cupboard between the kitchen and the dining area.

**Dividing with decoration** If you want to keep what little space you have open-plan, but need to give definition to the individual areas within it, the best solution is to divide your interior visually, by decorating each area differently. Use a different kind of flooring, for example, for the sitting zone and the eating zone; paint the walls of the work space in a different color from those of the dining area beside it. In this way, you can create the impression of rooms without the need for dividing walls or partitions.

A neutral color scheme can work well in a small home. It makes the most of the light, and if you choose warm natural colors, as here, it can add a touch of softness to an otherwise hard-edged space. Don't feel you have to stick to one shade, however. By using contrasting tones, you can effectively divide up an open-plan space without the need for walls. Here, a large deep cream artwork defines the dining area.

# color, texture, & lighting

Few of us have the luxury of building our own homes or even adapting them, but we can all personalize our living spaces with decoration. This interior discipline used to be just that—disciplined—but today we can do whatever we like within our own four walls. Freed from the constraints and conventions of traditional interior design, we can paint our bedrooms fuchsia pink and our kitchens deep purple; we can cover our floors with stainless steel and our walls with bamboo; we can flood our bathrooms with colored light.

Decoration is more than just self-expression, however. In addition to changing the esthetics of our interiors, it can do much to alter the dynamics of the space itself. A color can change the mood of a room; a pattern seem to alter its proportions; and lighting, cleverly placed, can camouflage its dimensions. These pragmatic effects of decoration are particularly valuable when you are trying to make a small home seem bigger, of course, especially if your budget is limited (decorative work usually costs a fraction of the price of structural changes). So, before you decide on a decorative scheme, play around with color, texture, and pattern (sample pots and swatches come in handy here) to make sure you are really going to make the most of your space.

## COLOR

Color is, without doubt, the most expressive of decorating tools and often the hardest to get right. With so much choice, it can be difficult to know just which shades to choose, particularly in a small home where there is little space for mistakes. If you need some help, there are, of course, a host of well-meaning experts to consult and countless decorating principles telling you which colors should go where, but really the best advice is to browse through magazines and paint charts, choose a

ABOVE **With its subtle mix of soft pastel colors and its sweep of sleek wooden floor, this interior feels very open and cohesive. The parchment** tone of the walls has been picked up in the furniture and in the giant artwork, making the whole space hang together perfectly.

color you like, and try it out. Be adventurous. Many small-home owners stick to a neutral palette in the belief that pale colors will make their space seem larger (a half-truth at best), but there is room for bold color in a small area if you use it wisely and imaginatively. A tiny room painted vivid red or deep blue, for example, will be far more striking and memorable than yet another pale cream one (remember, though, that sunlight can change color dramatically, so the dark red you pick out in the paint store might turn into brilliant crimson in a sunny bedroom). One good tip is to paint the ceiling of a room a few shades darker than the walls so that, in a very tiny space, the latter won't seem oppressive and the former should seem to recede.

**All white** The all-white look can work well in a tiny space, for it will make the perimeter of any room "disappear," and of course, it will make the most of the light. Be careful, however, to take the edge off a white interior by introducing soft and comfortable elements in the furniture or furnishings to prevent the space from becoming too cold and clinical. Also, try to add some very personal pieces to the mix to stop it from looking bland.

**Gradations of color** Using a series of deepening colors is a good way to suggest depth of space in a tiny area, and it can look very effective, too. Paint a panel of your chosen color on a wall and then use the colors it sits next to on the paint chart (in other words, a tone lighter and a tone darker) on each side. In addition to working on a small scale within one room, this can also be done on a larger scale, so the living room, say, would be painted the first color, the adjacent room, in the next, and so on throughout the house. An added advantage of this technique is that by using varying tones of the same color throughout your home, you will visually

Take the edge off a white interior by introducing soft and comfortable elements to prevent the space from becoming too cold and clinical. Also, add some very personal pieces to the mix to stop it from looking bland.

blur the internal boundaries and give a sense of cohesion to the whole space.

**Introducing bold color** You can see from the first part of this book just how tempting it is to use a neutral, monochrome palette in a small space, but most of these home owners have added a dash of vivid color to perk their interiors up a bit (those vivid green carpets in Helen Ellery's tiny urban terrace, for example). The key is to use bright color subtly and cohesively (you don't want four clashing walls

fighting for attention in a tiny room) and to intersperse bold colors with white to give each the space to breathe.

By using strong and differing tones throughout your interior, you can also cleverly manipulate the sense of space, for the eye will be drawn through a doorway or internal window if a contrasting color (or two) can be spied through it. Glimpsing green, say, or green and purple through a yellow archway, for example, will give you a far stronger sense of the space beyond than if everything were white.

It is tempting to opt for a neutral palette in a small space to make the most of the light, and it can work well. Don't feel you have to play too safe, however. The odd splash of brilliance, such as the vivid red lampshade and richly colored painting here, can make a room.

If you don't want to go for color in the structure of your home, add it in the furnishings instead, but remember that a vivid sofa will stand out far more forcibly if its surroundings are pale.

## TEXTURE AND PATTERN

**Materials and finishes** Color, as we know, can have a dramatic effect on the spatial qualities of a room, but how many of us think about the role that a paint finish or a flooring material can play in the same way? We tend to choose these for looks or price alone without considering their impact on the sense of space. The thing to remember is that any reflective surface will increase the light and make a room seem larger. So opt—if you can—for the shiny and the glossy: a varnished resin floor, perhaps; stainless-steel kitchen units; gloss paint on the walls; and mirrors, well, wherever you can put them (the bathroom ceiling is a good place, see page 31). In this way, you can get the very structure of your home to double your space.

**Pattern** Even the plainest home has pattern—the crisscross geometry of a wall of tiles; the line of a baseboard; the ridges on a sweep of natural flooring—and in a small home it stands out far more than in a large one. Because any strong linear pattern can play havoc with our sense of perspective (think of a Bridget Riley painting), it is particularly important to make sure that whatever pattern you have works with your space rather than against it. Here are a few general rules:

• Avoid striped wallpaper: too many vertical lines will make the walls close in and make a room feel claustrophobic. If you must have stripes, go for one or two horizontals instead (though if painted right around a room, this can also have a constricting effect).

• Never let vertical lines overpower the horizontals: a long, low bench, for example, will do far more to extend a room than tall, thin bookcases.

• Don't tile a bathroom completely. The grid of the grout (or even just the seams of the tiles) will be overpowering in a small space.

• Try to create a strong diagonal focus across your interior (a change of flooring or cannily positioned furniture can help to achieve this), for this will encourage the eye to scan the longest sweep of space.

As for more superimposed decorative pattern, feel free to make it big (overblown flowers on a wallpaper, say) because, perversely, this can make a room seem larger. Use it sparingly, however (just on one wall, perhaps), or it can overcrowd a space. Small patterns can work well, but, again, be subtle unless you want an itsy-bitsy cottage look. Above all, choose a pattern you like: anything can work in a small space as long as it is not overdone.

## LIGHTING

Light can manipulate space more effectively than any other medium, making even a tiny area feel bigger than it really is. If your home has good natural light, make the most of it by adding windows or skylights if you need to, and by decking out your interior with reflective surfaces. If your home is on the dark side, however, don't despair. Even the brightest home needs a supplement of artificial lighting, and you can just up the quota of bulbs, tubes, and directional spots to suit your needs. How much light you require will depend on the weather, the time of day, the season, and so on, so try to build flexibility into your system, so you can change the mood of your lighting at the flick of a switch. And introduce a mixture of different kinds of light (cool fluorescents and warm tungstens, for example) so you can create the atmosphere you want when you want it. These days, artificial light can do everything from replicating daylight to making your furniture "float," so even the darkest, tiniest interior can be transformed with light.

**Dividing with light** A good way of defining different areas within a small space without the need for physical partitions is to light them differently. If you have a combined living and dining room, for example, you could isolate the eating area with a series of downlighters (on dimmers, perhaps) and give the rest of the room a wash of warm ambient light.

**Space-suggesting lighting** Light can do much to increase our perception of space if it is cleverly positioned. In the past, we all made do with a solitary pendant or a series of table lamps to light our rooms—downlighting solutions that could only make space seem smaller and more confining. Today, there is a vast choice of light designs on the market, from uplighters to wall-washers, and, installed carefully, many of them can make a room seem larger instantly. Take a look at what is on offer, get advice from the experts, and pick a system that will work in your particular interior. Here are a few ideas:

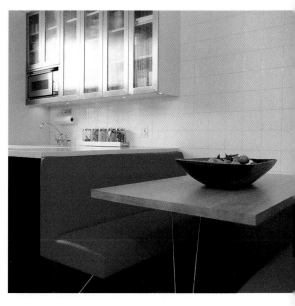

Hidden lighting can transform the sense of space in any small room, whether it is placed beneath wall-mounted furniture (OPPOSITE AND ABOVE), or placed around the edges of a false ceiling to make it "float" (BELOW). Here, though the source is concealed, the wall is washed with light. A glowing ball, tucked into a dark corner (LEFT), can also transform a compact room.

• Uplighters or angled spotlights can bounce light off a wall or a ceiling, which will make these surfaces seem to open out rather than close in.

• A run of spotlights along a corridor floor (or a ceiling) will lead the eye away from the immediate environment and on into the adjacent space.

• Using hidden lighting is, perhaps, the most effective way of suggesting continuing space. A row of kitchen units or a floor-to-ceiling cupboard illuminated at top and bottom by concealed neon strips, for example, will seem to float in the pool of light and become, thus, less of a barrier (see pages 10–17). A backlit bathroom mirror or cabinet will similarly seem to have more space behind it than it really does.

Artificial light can replicate daylight and make furniture "float," so the darkest interior can be transformed with light.

# storage, display, & furniture

The 21st-century home has become a refuge from the stressful and frenetic world outside, and it should, the magazines tell us, be calm, comfortable, and clutter-free. The image of the perfect modern interior with its sweeps of empty space is an easy one to aspire to, but it can be hard to create it for ourselves, particularly—of course—in a small home. Packed with furniture, furnishings, and an ever-growing hoard of possessions (clothes, toys, bedding, tableware… need I go on?), the tiny home can easily become overrun with clutter.

There are steps you can take, however, to redress the situation. The first is to be brutal and pare down your possessions (many of us have far too much stuff anyway). The second is to buy only what you need (those fashionable must-haves will look dated in no time). The third, and most important, is to store what you have effectively so you can keep your clutter under control, too.

Although most of us crave an ordered, well-organized living space, we don't want our homes to be regimented machines for living in. We need them, instead, to be personal, individual places, and this is where display comes in. By dealing with the mess and gaining control of our surroundings, we then have the luxury of deciding which of our possessions to show off and which to keep hidden. After all, those newly cleared counters and shelves will make perfect display space.

## STORAGE
OK, so it's down to the nitty gritty. If you don't have an attic or a cellar, where can you put your winter clothes and boots? If you have only a teeny-weeny kitchen, where can you stash all your utensils and tableware? Storage is talked of as the great decluttering solution, but where, in a tiny home, is there the space for it?

Well, you'd be surprised. Alongside the obvious freestanding solutions—the cupboard, the chest of drawers, the filing cabinet—there are also countless potential storage spots around the home just waiting to be exploited. Under the cooktop, above the fridge, inside the stairs: such wasted and awkward spaces can be converted into ingenious built-in storage. Supplement them with the odd freestanding piece, and you should find that you have far more room for putting things than you ever thought you had.

**Built-in** If you are building a brand-new interior, incorporate as much storage space as you can into the architecture of your home. You can never have too much. Built-in closets are standard, of course, but think of other ways of introducing hiding space into the fabric of a room. Create a seamless wall of floor-to-ceiling cupboards, for example, on one side of a room. Keep the doors plain and unfussy (with push-open latches rather than handles) and, when closed, the cupboards will disappear into the structure of the space. Alternatively, create a false wall at one end of a room (or wherever you can) and use the space within for shallow shelves, or increase the thickness of a door or partition to make a narrow hiding place inside. Think, too, about exploiting dead space. Stack triangular shelves into an unused corner or build a cupboard above a doorway or underneath a basin.

Storage comes in all shapes and sizes, but the main thing to remember is that you can't have too much of it. Mix and match whatever you like, from traditional closets (OPPOSITE) to more contemporary open shelving solutions (LEFT). Piled-up clothes and clutter can look messy in a small space, so get your storage units built in if you can or, alternatively, conceal them with a screen or a simple curtain (BELOW).

Built-in storage is the least visible of all storage solutions, but don't be tempted to overdo it. Consider the proportions of a room before you start. A wall of cupboards may look sleek and streamlined, but in a very narrow room, they might encroach too much on the space, and a freestanding solution may be better. Think carefully about your individual requirements and try to come up with a solution that works with your space rather than against it.

**Unexpected storage** If you haven't the room for conventional built-in storage solutions, consider more unlikely places to conceal your clutter. Take a good look around your home and assess any wasted space. Could you squeeze a hiding place underneath the stove or behind the bathroom mirror? Would a shallow drawer fit beneath a counter? Consider, too, the less obvious solutions. You could raise the level of the floor, for example, in one part of your home (see Dividing Space,

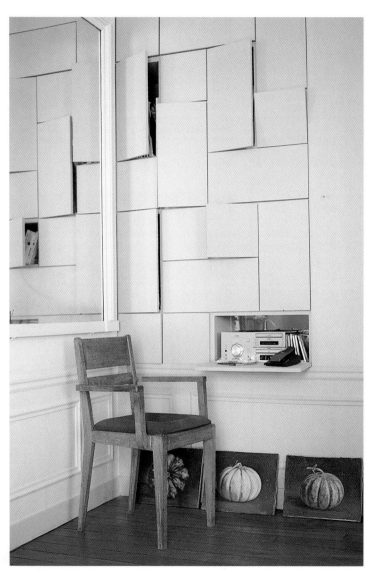

LEFT **This fantastic Advent-calendar-like storage system has been built, unobtrusively, into a cavity along the wall so it doesn't take up central space. Designed with various different-sized cupboards, it can accommodate all manner of things. Also, with a mirror hung on the wall on one side, it seems twice the size.**

ABOVE RIGHT AND CENTER **Any dead space can be used for storage. Here, the area under a spiral staircase has been turned into a wardrobe area with a clothes rod.**

OPPOSITE, BELOW LEFT AND RIGHT **Placed on a mezzanine platform, this tiny dressing area has mirrored cupboards to make it look bigger.**

page 117) and use the area for stashing bulky things such as boxes of old books or ski equipment. You may be able to dig out a storage area underground (this would be ideal for a wine cellar). You could even store things inside the stairs (see below).

Wherever you decide to create extra storage space, think carefully about how you will use it. While the things you rarely use can be stowed high up or right at the back of a cupboard, those you need regularly should be easily accessible.

**Stair storage** For most of us, stairs do no more than lead from one floor to the next, but in a small house they can fulfill a far more significant role by providing stacks of storage space. We are all familiar with the "cupboard under the stairs," which can be used to house anything from the vacuum to the fridge (see pages 10–17), but few of us exploit the storage potential of the steps themselves. Filled with drawers (accessed from the risers

at the front) or storage boxes (accessed from the tread, which can be hinged to make things easier), they provide great secret stashing space for anything from shoes to box files.

**The storage wall** Turning an entire wall into a storage system can be a clever solution in a small home (particularly if you can use a wall that would otherwise be redundant). By providing a home for all sorts of possessions —from books and CDs to bigger items such as audiovisual gear—it will free floor space elsewhere and, contained in just one area, will give a sleek, streamlined feel to the interior. If your budget is big enough, get the system custommade so that each compartment will be a perfect fit for your possessions, and choose a combination of closed cupboards

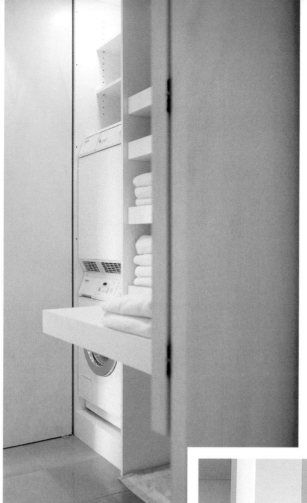

Freestanding pieces are, by contrast, extremely adaptable: you can reposition an armoire; you can sell it; you can move it to a different room and you won't need to get the builders in to sort it out for you. Consider your individual situation and choose the kind of storage options that will suit you and your home. A combination of built-in and freestanding is often the best solution.

*See overleaf for details on storage furniture and also see the individual chapters of The Zones for further storage ideas.*

If you are building a brand-new interior, incorporate as much storage as you can into the architecture of your home. You can never have too much.

and open pigeonholes, thereby creating space for both storage and display.

For inspiration, take a look at the sleek wood-veneered storage wall in Mark Rabiner and Avi Pemper's New York apartment (pages 24–31) and Paul Daly's flexible system in the Barbican (pages 52–59).

**Freestanding** Although creating built-in storage makes sense in a small home, it is worth bearing in mind that it isn't a flexible solution. You won't be able to move that built-in cupboard around or take it away with you when you move. Building specific storage can also be a costly and lengthy process, and although you will reap the benefits in the long run, this is also something that you should take into account before you start.

**The best thing about getting custommade storage built into your home is that it can be tailormade to suit your needs.** A vast clothes collection can be housed in a wall of closets or a mini walk-in dressing room (see p58); books housed in shelves of just the right size (FAR LEFT); towels and bed linen stashed away in a unit built just for the purpose (ABOVE). Here a pull-out shelf has been included to make folding laundry easier.

RIGHT **Built-in boxes are brilliantly flexible and useful for both storage and display.**

## FURNITURE

Finding furniture to fit a small home can seem a big problem. Although it is fairly easy to cut down on the incidental pieces (who needs a china cabinet anyway?), we all need some essentials, and even accommodating these can seem an impossible task in a tiny space. A table and six dining chairs may make a mini eating area look cramped and overcrowded; even an average-sized sofa may dominate a small living room. So, what can be done?

It is tempting, of course, to rush out and buy diminutive furniture and fixtures. Although these can work well, particularly in utility rooms like the bathroom (see page 37), kitting your interior out with mini bits and pieces is not always the best solution. A tiny armchair might fit in the corner of your living room, but may highlight its diminutive dimensions. A small-scale bed may give you room to move in the bedroom but be impractical for sleeping. The best advice is to think very carefully about what you need and to consider all the alternatives. Rather than opting for conventional furniture, for example, you could incorporate a seating

ABOVE **Adaptable and modular furniture that can be reconfigured at whim is often the best solution in a tiny home.**

ABOVE LEFT AND LEFT **In a small space, invest in furniture that is dual-functional, like this headboard-cabinet.**

Show a small group of sculptural ceramics rather than filling your shelves with knick-knacks—and make your displays enlarge the perception of space.

or a sleeping solution into the very structure of your home (a mezzanine-bed, perhaps or a built-in shelf-bench). You could find a piece that would solve a space issue for you (a folding bed or a stool that turns into a table). You could do away with armchairs and sit on the floor. By thinking laterally and by taking a different approach to furnishing your home, you should be able to create an interior that's functional and comfortable without being stuffed with furniture.

**Built-in solutions**  Creating built-in furniture can be the best option in a small living space and works particularly well if you can create something that does two jobs at once. Rather than investing in armchairs, for example, run a long, low plinth along one of the living-room walls. This can then act as a shelf or a seat and provide room for stowing books or magazines underneath. Create your own built-in bed, and you can choose to sit it on top of a series of drawers so it offers sleeping space and extensive storage (see page 36). Built-in furniture won't be flexible in itself, but—paradoxically—it can make your interior flexible and get rid of the need for intrusive freestanding pieces.

**Keep it low**  Using low, horizontal furniture will instantly make an interior seem bigger, a phenomenon that the Japanese—experts at managing small spaces—have exploited very successfully with their shallow tables, futon beds, and tatami mats. By taking furniture down to floor level, you not only clear eye-level space (which in itself makes a room seem larger), but also extend the distance between yourself and the ceiling. Also, by opting for floor cushions, beanbags, and low benches rather than dining or armchairs that have legs, backs, and bulky bases, you will free up space and, at the same time, be at the cutting edge of contemporary living.

**Multipurpose pieces**  If you are investing in freestanding furniture, try to choose adaptable pieces that perform two or more functions. Pick a dining table that can double as a desk, a stool that has storage space inside, or a bookcase that can divide two different areas of a room. If your furniture is hard-working, you will—quite simply—need less of it.

**Storage furniture**  There's furniture specifically for storage, of course— armoires, linen chests, bookcases, and so on—but other pieces, too, can be customized to house your possessions. The hollow arms of a sofa could be made to hold CDs or videos; the underside of a tabletop fitted with narrow drawers for flatware; the bottom of a bed fitted with a storage area for blankets and sheets. With just a little lateral thinking, you can make use of the invisible dead space inside all your furniture and help keep your interior clutter-free.

**Adaptable and modular**  Flat-pack, foldaway, stackable, extendable, adjustable, mobile—these are the kind of qualities you should be looking for when you are furnishing a tiny home. What you want is furniture that is flexible: the chair that can be brought out for a guest and then packed away again; the table that can be one height for supper and another for coffee; the bed that can be extended; the stools that can, together, form a table; the kitchen island unit that can be wheeled to one side when not in use. Versatility and convenience are where it's at.

**See-through furniture** In a small space you need your freestanding furniture to be as unobtrusive as possible. Choose a design that won't block the light or create too much shadow. Tables and chairs in transparent materials (glass or Plexiglas) work well (see Guy Hills's kitchen on page 16), and pieces made of wire mesh will dominate less than solid pieces. Best of all, of course, choose mirrored furniture for your interior. Not only will it increase the light, but it will make your space seem bigger, too.

**Mini and maxi** Filling your tiny home with diminutive pieces of furniture will, obviously, give you more space, but don't be afraid of using the odd overscaled piece, too. A large item of furniture added to the mix—such as a vast railroad clock, for example (see Helen Ellery's dining area on page 35)—can give a quirky touch to a room and also make the atmosphere bigger, conning the eye into thinking there is more space than there really is.

### DISPLAY
Yes, I know you need to get rid of your clutter, but there is room for a spot of display in small homes. The key is to keep it simple—so show a small group of sculptural ceramics rather than filling your shelves with knick-knacks— and to think of ways of making your displays enlarge the perception of space.

**Diminishing scale** By displaying a series of objects in descending order of size, you can play visual tricks with the proportion of a room

In a small space, the few pieces of furniture you have will need to work twice as hard as normal. This funky corner sofa, for example, not only provides seats for the dining table and a shelf (at the back) for a telephone, it also contains huge storage drawers at one end. The sleek 1960s-look table, which cleverly wraps itself around the two curvy armchairs, also effectively saves space.

or just a piece of furniture. A nest of small tables displayed in a row rather than grouped together, for example, or a series of bottles, say, lined up in diminishing size against a wall can help to make a tiny room seem larger. Experiment with your possessions and see what difference a display can make.

**Tiny things** A display of small things can make a big impact in a tiny space, and if you choose your objects carefully, it needn't be twee. Line up a collection of keys on a wall, for example, or a series of tiny pictures, and you should make a graphic and eye-catching display, which (because there are multiple

elements to your arrangement) will help to extend the dimensions of a room.

**Where to do it** The main problem about arranging things in a small space is deciding where to do it, particularly if you have little freestanding furniture. Think laterally, however, and you should come up with a few potential display spots. You could prop pictures on the floor if you lack wall space, for example; use the edges of the stairs; or even hang things from the ceiling (a graphic mobile, perhaps). Wherever you decide to show off your possessions, don't overdo it. Less in a small house is very definitely more.

With just a little lateral thinking, you can make use of the invisible dead space inside all your furniture and help keep your interior clutter-free.

# resources

## ALL-ROUNDERS

### ABC Carpet & Home

881–888 Broadway
New York, NY 10003
212 674 1144
For a store near you, call
561 279 7777
www.abchome.com

*Home furnishings, fabrics, carpets, and design accessories.*

### Anthropologie

375 West Broadway
New York, NY
Call 800 309 2500 for your
nearest store
www.anthropologie.com

*Furniture and home furnishings.*

### The Conran Shop

407 East 59th Street
New York, NY 10022
212 755 9079
www.conran.com

*Cutting-edge design from furniture to forks.*

### Crate & Barrel

646 N Michigan Avenue
Chicago, IL 60611
800 996 9960
For a retailer near you, call
800 927 9202
www.crateandbarrel.com

*Good value furniture and accessories with great style.*

### IKEA

Potomac Mills Mall
2700 Potomac Circle
Suite 888
Woodbridge, VA 22192
For a store near you, call
847 969 9700 or
800 434 4532
www.ikea-usa.com

*Home basics at great prices, including assembly-kit furniture.*

### MOMA Design Store

44 West 53rd Street
New York, NY 10022
800 447 6662
www.momastore.org

*A finely honed selection of furniture, lighting, kitchen, and tabletop accessories by modern designers including Starck, Wright, and Vasa.*

### Pier One Imports

71 Fifth Avenue
New York, NY 10003
212 206 1911
www.pier1.com

*Home accessories and furniture.*

### Pottery Barn

P.O. Box 7044
San Francisco
CA 94120-7044
For a store near you, call
800 922 9934
www.potterybarn.com

*Everything from furniture to decoration details.*

### Restoration Hardware

935 Broadway
New York, NY 10011
212 260 9479
www.restoration
hardware.com

*Some of the funkiest home furnishings, lighting, and accessories you'll find.*

### Waverly

Dealer locations:
800 423 5881
www.waverly.com

*Decorative accessories including fabric, wallpaper, furniture, paint, window treatments, and flooring.*

## KITCHENS

### DuPont Corian®

Barley Mill Plaza
Price Mill Building
P.O. Box 80012
Wilmington, DE 19880
800 426 7426
www.dupont.com/corian/

*Nonporous acrylic surface for counters and sinks. Stains or scratches can easily be ground out.*

### iKitchenBath.com

738 Franklin Avenue, Suite B
Franklin Square
NY 11010
800 646 1305
lasalesco@aol.com
www.lasalesco.com

*Mini kitchens including compact kitchenettes incorporating refrigerator, burners and sink; tabletop dishwashers and compact washer/driers.*

### Imperial Cal Products

1141 S. Acacia Avenue
Fullerton CA 92831
714 446 7440
www.imperialhoods.com

*Under-hood lighting for kitchen countertops.*

## BATHROOMS

### Acme Brick Co.

P.O. Box 425
Fort Worth, TX 76101
800 932 2263

*Glass-block walls.*

### American Standard

P.O. Box 6820
1 Centennial Plaza
Piscataway NJ 08855-6820
Tel: 800-359-3261
www.american
standard-us.com

*Wall-mounted basins and other sanitaryware.*

### Butler Manufacturing Company

1540 Genessee
Kansas City MO 64102
816 968 3000
www.butlermfg.com

*Manufacturers of "intelligent" electro-polarizing glass (similar to that shown on page 93).*

### Epanel Inc.

P.O. Box 115
Pennington, NJ 08534
800 537 2635

*Electric towel warmers, towel bars, towel rings.*

### Just Options

633 Langdale Drive
Ft. Collins, CO 80526-3941
970 266 1907
www.just-options.com

*Wide selection of towel-rail and column radiators*

### Priva-lite

www.sggprivalite.com

*Electrically switchable obscured glass.*

### Tile Mosaics.com

8133 Firestone Boulevard
Downey CA 90241
562 904 8446
www.tilemosaics.com

*Supplier of mosaic tiles.*

## BEDS

### Carlyle Custom Convertibles

1375 Third Avenue
New York, NY 10028
212 570 326

*Convertible sofas.*

### Create-A-Bed

4735 Poplar Level Road
Suite 3
Louisville, KT 40213-2484
1 877 966 3852 (toll free)
info@wallbed.com
www.wallbed.com

*Kit wall beds to put together yourself.*

**Tiltaway**

1390 N. Rugby Road
Hendersonville, NC 28791
Toll free: (877) TILT-BED/
(877) 8458-233
beds@tiltaway.com
www.tiltaway.com

*Variety of wall beds.*

## STORAGE

**California Closets**

Call 888 336 9709 for a
store near you
www.calclosets.com

*Custom-made clothes
storage to fit your space.*

**Hold Everything**

P.O. Box 7807
San Francisco, CA 94120
800 840 3596
www.holdeverything.com

*Everything for storage from
baskets to shoe holders.*

**National Closet Group**

953 North Larch
Elmhurst, IL 60126
866 624 5463
www.nationalcloset
group.com

*Provides a network of the
best independent storage
design companies in the US.*

## SKYLIGHTS, WINDOWS, & WALLS

**Fisher Skylights**

5005 Veterans Memorial
Highway
Holbrook, NY 11741
800 431 1586
www.fisherskylights.com

*Metal-framed skylights, from
pre-designed modular
systems to custom-
engineered projects.*

**Kalwall**

1111 Candia Road
P.O. Box 237
Manchester, NH 03105
800 258 9777
info@kalwall.com
www.kalwall.com

*Wall systems, curtain walls,
windows, standard
skylights, pre-engineered
and custom skylights,
sloped glazing systems,
plastic unit skylights, and
translucent skylights.*

**Kolbe & Kolbe**

1323 S 11th Avenue
Wausau, WI 54401
For a retailer near you, call
800 955 8177

*Windows and doors.*

**Smith & Noble**

P.O. Box 1387
Corona, CA 91718
800 248 8888
www.smithandnoble.com

*Vertical and horizontal
shades and blinds in
all materials, Roman
shades, cornice boxes.
Mail order. Catalog.*

**Velux America Inc.**

P.O. Box 5001
Greenwood, SC 29648
800 88 VELUX
www.velux-america.com

*Velux windows and skylights.*

**Wausau Window & Wall**

1415 West Street
Wausau, WI 54401
715 845 2161 or
877 678 2983
www.wausau
windows.com

*Custommade windows and
curtain walls, projected/
casement windows, ribbon/
strip windows, double- or
single-hung, sliding doors,
and horizontal sliders.*

## LIGHTING

**Kichler Lighting Group**

7711 East Pleasant
Valley Road
Cleveland, OH 44131
800 659 9000
216 573 1000
www.kichler.com

*Any type of lighting,including
under-counter fluorescents.*

**Lumax Industries Inc.**

Chestnut Avenue &
4th Street
Altona, PA 16603
814 944 2537

*Fluorescent lighting.*

## HEATING

**Comfort Glow Heating
Products**

1251 Mound Avenue
Grand Rapids, MI 49504
616 791 7325
www.comfortglow.com

*Fire boxes, inset fireplaces,
radiant flame heaters, and
much more.*

## FLOORING

**Advance Terrazzo Inc.**

1217 East Gibson Lane
Phoenix, AZ 85034
800 323 9736 or
602 253 9400
www.advance
terrazzo.com

*With over 50 marble, glass,
and plastic aggregates, they
can match any paint coloring
when laying chips in resin
flooring (for a look similar to
Guy Hills's), or create
specific mosaic designs.*

**Classic Tile Inc.**

325 Pine Street
Elizabeth, NJ 07206
908 289 8400
www.classictile.com

*Installers and distributors of
Estrie and Flexco textured
rubber flooring, as well as
Anderson hardwood,
Congoleum, Formica,
Wicander vinyl-clad cork,
poured rubber floors, and
many other quality resilient
flooring surfaces.*

## STRUCTURAL SOLUTIONS

**American Society of
Heating, Refrigeration,
and Air Conditioning
Engineers Inc.**

17191 Tullie Circle NE
Atlanta, GA 30329-3025
404 636 8400
www.ashrae.org

**National Construction
Estimator**

www.get-a-quote.net

*Labor and material cost
estimates for residential,
commercial, or industrial
construction projects.*

**Your Complete Home**

www.yourcomplete
home.com

*Provides listings for
contractors in every state, as
well as helpful information
about financing, hiring, and
do-it-yourself projects.*

# architects & designers

whose work is featured in this book

**AB Construction**

Contractor
31 Aldbourne Road
London W12 OLW
UK
t. +44 (20) 8749 2044

*Pages 96–97, 113 a*

**Bruce Bierman Design, Inc.**

29 West 15 Street
New York NY 10011
t. 212 243 1935
f. 212 243 6615
w. www.biermandesign.com

*Pages 81, 93 br, 107 a, 113 b,
130–131 a*

**Tito Canella**

Canella & Achilli Architects
via Revere # 7/9
20123 Milano
Italy
t. +39 02 46 95 222
f. +39 02 48 13 704
e. ac@planet.it
w. www.canella-achilli.com

*Pages 1–2, 68–69, 71 br, 74, 82, 98
r–99, 113 c, 116, 128 r–129, 131 b*

**Paul Collier**

Architect
209 rue St Maur
75010 Paris
France
t. +33 1 53 72 49 32
e. paul.collier@architecte.net

*Pages 6, 75, 79, 102*

**Fabienne Couvert
Guillaume Terver**

cxt sarl d'architecture
12 rue Saint Fiacre
75002 Paris
France
t. +33 1 55 34 9850
f. +33 1 55 34 9849
w. www.couverterver-
    architectes.com

*Pages 4–5, 60–65*

**d-squared design**

6b Blackbird Yard
Ravenscroft Street
London E2 7RP
UK
t. +44 (20) 7739 2632
f. +44 (20) 7739 2633
e. dsquared@globalnet.co.uk

*Pages 96–97, 113 a*

**David Mikhail Architects**

Unit 29
1–13 Adler Street
London E1 1EE
UK
t. +44 (20) 7377 8424
f. +44 (20) 7377 5791
w. www.davidmikhail.com

*Page 91 r*

**Dune, Inc.**

Furniture Fabrication
88 Franklin Street
New York NY 10013
t. 212 925 6171

*Pages 24–31*

**Helen Ellery**

The Plot London
Interior Design
77 Compton Street
London EC1V OBN
UK
t. +44 (20) 7251 8116
f. +44 (20) 7251 8117
e. helen@theplotlondon.com
w. www.theplotlondon.com

*Pages 32–37, 73 r, endpapers*

**Gavin Jackson Architects**

t. (07050) 097561

*Pages 66–67, 70 b, 78, 98 l*

**Guy Hills**

Photographer
t. +44 (20) 7916 2610
m. 07831 548068
e. guyhills@hotmail.com

*Pages 10–17*

**Interior Concepts**

6 Warren Hall
Manor Road
Loughton
Essex IG10 4RP
UK
t. +44 (20) 8508 9952
f. +44 (20) 8502 4382
m. 07796 305133
e. jo_interiorconcepts
    @hotmail.com
w. www.jointeriorconcepts.co.uk

*Pages 4 l, 71 l, 72–73 l, 101 r, 109,
125 al, 134–135*

**Jonathan Clark Architects**

t. +44 (20) 7286 5676
f. +44 (20) 7490 8530
e. jonathan@jonathan
    clarkarchitects.co.uk

*Pages 8–9, 38–45*

**Clark Johnson**

Lighting Consultant
Johnson Schwinghammer
335 West 38th Street
New York NY 10018
t. 212 643 1552

*Pages 24–31*

**Joseph Kerwin**

Garden Consultant
La Buona Terra, Inc.
261 West 22nd Street
New York NY 10011
t. 212 229 2268

*Pages 24–31*

**David Khouri**

Comma
Architecture, Interiors & Furniture
149 Wooster Street
Suite 4NW
New York, NY 10012
t. 212 420 7866
f. 212 202 3584
e. info@comma-nyc.com
w. www.comma-nyc.com

*Pages 24–31*

**Lloyd Schwan/Design**

195 Chrystie Street, # 908
New York NY 10002
t. 212 375 0858
f. 212 375 0887
e. lloydschwan@earthlink.net

*Pages 114–115, 132–133*

**Mullman Seidman Architects**

Architecture & Interior Design
443 Greenwich Street, # 2A
New York NY 10013
t. 212 431 0770
f. 212 431 8428
e. msa@mullmanseidman.com

*Pages 80 a & bl, 83, 86–87, 94*

**François Muracciole**

Architect
54 rue de Montreuil
75011 Paris
France
t. +33 1 43 71 33 03
e. francois.muracciole
  @libertysurf.fr

*Page 128 l*

**Paul Daly Design Studio Ltd**

11 Hoxton Square
London N1 6NU
UK
t. +44 (20) 7613 4855
f. +44 (20) 7613 5848
e. studio@pauldaly.com
w. www.pauldaly.com

*Pages 3, 52–59*

**Retrouvius Reclamation
& Design**

32 York House
Upper Montagu Street
London W1H 1FR
UK
t./f. +44 (20) 7724 3387
m. 07778 210855

*Pages 10–17*

**Sage Wimer Coombe
Architects**

480 Canal Street, Room 1002
New York NY 10013
t. 212 226 9600

*Page 88*

**Carla Saibene**

Womenswear collection,
accessories and antiques
Shop:
Carla Saibene
via San Maurilio 20
Milano
Italy
t./f. +39 2 77 33 15 70
e. xaibsrl@yahoo.com

*Pages 85, 100–101, 118–119,
126–127 a, 144*

**Seth Stein Architects**

15 Grand Union Centre
West Row
Ladbroke Grove
London W10 5AS
UK
t. +44 (20) 8968 8581
f. +44 (20) 8968 8591
e. admin@sethstein.com

*Page 93 ar & cr*

**Shamir Shah**

e. shahdesign@earthlink.net

*Pages 46–51*

**Site Specific Ltd**

60 Peartree Street
London EC1V 3SB
UK
t. +44 (20) 7490 3176
f. +44 (20) 7490 3427
e. office@sitespecificltd.co.uk
w. www.sitespecificltd.co.uk

*Pages 84, 90–91, 103, 125 b, 130 l*

**Nigel Smith**

t. +44 (20) 7278 8802
e. n-smith@dircon.co.uk

*Page 93 ac*

**Steven Learner Studio**

307 Seventh Avenue
New York NY 10001
t. 212 741 8583
f. 212 741 2180
w. www.stevenlearnerstudio.com

*Page 125 ar*

**Bruno Tanquerel**

Artist
2 Passage St Sébastien
75011 Paris
France
t. +33 1 43 57 03 93

*Pages 92–93*

**Todd Klein, Inc.**

27 West 24th Street, Suite 802
New York NY 10010
t. 212 414 0001
f. 212 414 1444
e. todd@toddklein.com

*Pages 110–112, 122–123, 127 b*

**27.12 Design Ltd**

333 Hudson Street
10th Floor
New York NY 10014
t. 212 727 8169
w. www.2712design.com

*Pages 106, 107 b, 120–121,
132 l & b*

**USE Architects**

11 Northburgh Street
London EC1V 0AH
UK
t. +44 (20) 7251 5559
f. +44 (20) 7253 5558
e. use.arch@virgin.net

*Pages 89, 117, 124*

**Woodhams Landscape Ltd**

378 Brixton Road
London SW9 7AW
UK
t. +44 (20) 7346 5656
f. +44 (20) 7346 5646
e. stephen@woodhams.co.uk
w. www.woodhams.co.uk

Showroom:
One Aldwych
London WC2 4BZ
UK
t. +44 (20) 7300 0777
f. +44 (20) 7300 0778

*Pages 70 a, 76–77, 80 br, 104–105,
108*

With thanks to:

**Hurford Salvi Carr**

37–41 St John Street
London EC1M 4AN
UK
t. +44 (20) 7250 1012
f. +44 (20) 7490 1122
e. sales@h-s-c.co.uk
w. www.hurford-salvi-carr.co.uk

# picture credits

all photography by Chris Everard

KEY: **a** = above, **b** = below, **r** = right, **l** = left, **c** = center.

**Front and back endpapers:** A house in London designed by Helen Ellery of The Plot London; **1–2** An apartment in Milan designed by Tito Canella of Canella & Achilli Architects; **3** Yuen-Wei Chew's apartment in London designed by Paul Daly Design Studio Ltd; **4 l** Jo Warman – Interior Concepts; **4–5** An apartment in Paris designed by architects Guillaume Terver and Fabienne Couvert of cxt sarl d'architecture; **6** An apartment in Paris designed by architect Paul Collier; **8–9** Architect Jonathan Clark's home in London; **10–17** Photographer Guy Hills's house in London designed by Joanna Rippon and Maria Speake of Retrouvius; **18–23** Ben Atfield's house in London; **24–31** Pemper and Rabiner home in New York, designed by David Khouri of Comma; **32–37** A house in London designed by Helen Ellery of The Plot London, paintings by Robert Clarke; **38–45** Architect Jonathan Clark's home in London; **46–51** A New York apartment designed by Shamir Shah. Paintings, Artist Malcolm Hill; **52–59** Yuen-Wei Chew's apartment in London designed by Paul Daly Design Studio Ltd. Paintings by Carol Robertson; **60–65** An apartment in Paris designed by architects Guillaume Terver and Fabienne Couvert of cxt sarl d'architecture; **66–67** A London apartment designed by architect Gavin Jackson; **68–69 l** An apartment in Milan designed by Tito Canella of Canella & Achilli Architects; **69 c & r** Adèle Lakhdari's home in Milan; **70 a** Florist and landscape designer Stephen Woodhams's home in London, designed by architect Taylor Hammond; **70 b** A London apartment designed by architect Gavin Jackson; **71 br** An apartment in Milan designed by Tito Canella of Canella & Achilli Architects; **71 l & 72–73 l** Jo Warman – Interior Concepts; **73 r** A house in London designed by Helen Ellery of The Plot London; **74** An apartment in Milan designed by Tito Canella of Canella & Achilli Architects; **75** An apartment in Paris, designed by architect Paul Collier; **76–77** Florist and landscape designer Stephen Woodhams's home in London, designed by architect Taylor Hammond. Kitchen by Camarque, dog sculpture by Justine Smith; **78** A London apartment designed by architect Gavin Jackson; **79** An apartment in Paris designed by architect Paul Collier; **80 a** John Kifner's apartment in New York, designed by Mullman Seidman Architects; **80 bl** Peter and Nicole Dawes's apartment, designed by Mullman Seidman Architects; **80 br** Florist and landscape designer Stephen Woodhams's home in London, designed by architect Taylor Hammond; **81** Central Park West Residence, New York City designed by Bruce Bierman Design, Inc.; **82** An apartment in Milan designed by Tito Canella of Canella & Achilli Architects; **83** Peter and Nicole Dawes's apartment, designed by Mullman Seidman Architects; **84** An actor's London home designed by Site Specific; **85** Fashion designer Carla Saibene's home in Milan; **86–87** An apartment in New York, designed by Mullman Seidman Architects; **88** Bob & Maureen Macris' apartment on Fifth Avenue in New York designed by Sage Wimer Coombe Architects; **89** An apartment in London designed by Jo Hagan of Use Architects; **90–91** An actor's London home designed by Site Specific; **91 r** Simon Brignall & Christina Rosetti's loft apartment in London designed by David Mikhail Architects; **92–93** An apartment in Paris designed by Bruno Tanquerel; **93 ac** Architect Nigel Smith's apartment in London; **93 ar & cr** John Eldridge's loft apartment in London designed by Seth Stein; **93 br** Fifth Avenue Residence, New York City designed by Bruce Bierman Design, Inc.; **94** Monique Witt and Steven Rosenblum's apartment in New York, designed by Mullman Seidman Architects; **95** One New Inn Square, a private dining room and home of chef David Vanderhook, all enquiries 020 7729 3645; **96–97** Programmable House in London, designed by d-squared; **98 l** A London apartment designed by architect Gavin Jackson; **98 r–99** An apartment in Milan designed by Tito Canella of Canella & Achilli Architects; **100–101** Fashion designer Carla Saibene's home in Milan; **101 r** Jo Warman – Interior Concepts; **102** An apartment in Paris, designed by architect Paul Collier; **103** An actor's London home designed by Site Specific; **104–105** Florist and landscape designer Stephen Woodhams's home in London, designed by architect Taylor Hammond; **106 & 107 b** Apartment of Amy Harte Hossfeld and Martin Hossfeld; **107 a** Central Park West Residence, New York City designed by Bruce Bierman Design, Inc.; **108** Florist and landscape designer Stephen Woodhams's home in London, designed by architect Taylor Hammond; **109** Jo Warman – Interior Concepts; **110–112** Todd Klein's New York apartment designed by Todd Klein, Inc.; **113 a** Programmable House in London, designed by d-squared; **113 c** An apartment in Milan designed by Tito Canella of Canella & Achilli Architects; **113 b** Central Park West Residence, New York City designed by Bruce Bierman Design, Inc.; **114–115** Mark Weinstein's apartment in New York designed by Lloyd Schwan; **116** Adèle Lakhdari's home in Milan; **117** An apartment in London designed by Jo Hagan of Use Architects; **118–119** Fashion designer Carla Saibene's home in Milan; **120–121** Apartment of Amy Harte Hossfeld and Martin Hossfeld; **122–123** Todd Klein's New York apartment designed by Todd Klein, Inc.; **124** An apartment in London designed by Jo Hagan of Use Architects; **125 al** Jo Warman – Interior Concepts; **125 ar** An apartment in New York designed by Steven Learner; **125 b** An actor's London home designed by Site Specific; **126–127 a** Fashion designer Carla Saibene's home in Milan; **127 b** Todd Klein's New York apartment designed by Todd Klein, Inc.; **128 l** François Muracciole's apartment in Paris; **128 r–129** An apartment in Milan designed by Tito Canella of Canella & Achilli Architects; **130 l** An actor's London home designed by Site Specific; **130–131 a** Central Park West Residence, New York City designed by Bruce Bierman Design, Inc.; **131 b** An apartment in Milan designed by Tito Canella of Canella & Achilli Architects; **132 l & b** Apartment of Amy Harte Hossfeld and Martin Hossfeld; **132–133** Mark Weinstein's apartment in New York designed by Lloyd Schwan; **134–135** Jo Warman – Interior Concepts; **144** Fashion designer Carla Saibene's home in Milan.

The author would like to thank Azby Brown for information about Japanese design.

# index

page numbers in *italic* refer to captions and illustrations